Montpelier CHRONICLES

Montpelier CHRONICLES

Historic Stories of the Capital City

Paul Heller

The History Press

Published by The History Press
Charleston, SC 29403
www.historypress.net

First published 2015

Manufactured in the United States

ISBN 978.1.46711.857.6

Library of Congress Control Number: 2015945087

Contents

Introduction 7

How Montpelier Got Its Name: The Settlement of Montpelier and Place Name Origins 9
Chester Wright: Montpelier's First Minister Describes the Moral Climate of the Early Days 17
Common Crackers: The Famous Vermont Common Cracker's Origins in Montpelier 24
Sam Upham: Civil War Counterfeiter 31
Daniel Pierce Thompson: Montpelier's First Historian and Great Eccentric 38
The Montpelier Fire: The Great Fire of 1875 Determined the Appearance of the City 46
The Lane Shops: Important Manufacturer of the Nineteenth Century 55
Joel Foster and the Waterworks: The New Water System Introduced after the Great Fire 63
Gould-Caswell Murder: The "Montpelier Murder" of 1889 Made National News 71
Black Agnes: John Hubbard's Unquiet Grave 79
The Keeley Institute: Treating Substance Abuse at the Turn of the Century 87

Contents

Clang, Clang, Clang Went the Trolley: A Brief History of the Electric Railroad Between Barre and Montpelier 95
Emma Goldman and Montpelier's Socialist Hall: Anarchists in the Capital City, circa 1905 110
Dorman B.E. Kent: Montpelier Historian and Humorist 115
Montpelier's New Firehouse, 1924: The Consequences of a Tragic Fire 124
Mari Tomasi: The Montpelier Novelist Who Told Vermont's "Italian Story" 132

About the Author 141

Introduction

I am glad to have the opportunity to write a book about my hometown. I came to Montpelier as a boy and found a wonderful little city on a perfect scale for young adventure. Years later, living in nearby Barre, I became fascinated with local history, and after several years reading and writing about the Granite City, I have broadened my horizons to include Montpelier. Luckily for me, the *Times-Argus* newspaper has seen fit to publish my local history pieces, and most of these stories first appeared there. These sixteen essays represent a good sampling of Montpelier's history in the nineteenth and twentieth centuries.

In due time, I discovered the riches of Daniel Pierce Thompson's *History of Montpelier* and delighted in the wry observations of Dorman Kent, whose witty newspaper columns have been collected by my Montpelier High School classmate Mike Doyle. I kept Mike's *Events of This Day* and the Thompson volume close at hand when considering the pieces for this collection. Perry Merrill's chronology of Montpelier was also an essential ready reference. Mr. Merrill's grandson, Ed Otis, is another of my MHS classmates. It is hard to believe we will soon celebrate the fiftieth anniversary of our graduation.

I am fortunate to live close to the Vermont History Center on Washington Street in Barre. Its manuscripts, printed sources and photo archives are matched only by the extraordinary skill and expertise of its librarians, Paul Carnahan and Marjorie Strong, whose assistance in assembling images and manuscripts was indispensible. Images from its collection are indicated with the initials VHS; those from my collection bear the designation PH.

PAUL HELLER
Barre, 2015

How Montpelier Got Its Name

The Settlement of Montpelier and Place Name Origins

"What's in a name?" mused Juliet. "That which we call a rose by any other name would smell as sweet." Jacob Davis, the first settler of what was to become Vermont's permanent capital, strongly disagreed. He named his new town "Montpelier," eschewing the habit of giving a village the same name as the one that the first settlers had most recently abandoned. Instead, Davis chose to honor France, which had stood by the rebellious colonies in their defiance of England.

Think about it. The Green Mountains are rife with place names borrowed from Massachusetts and Connecticut. There is Guilford in the south, Canaan in the north, Hartford in the east, Manchester in the west and countless others in between. This practice was never more notably followed than in the naming of Barre, where champions of the two Massachusetts towns of Holden and Barre vied in a wrestling match for the honor of designating the new settlement with the name of the town from which they had emigrated. Finally, these place names often have antecedents in England, and my British friend Kevin Halford is vexed by the fact that these places, familiar to him, clearly have the wrong geographical relationship from that which he is accustomed. "It's all wrong, Paul," he opined.

Jacob Davis, one of the original 1781 charter holders for the new village and its first surveyor, wanted to honor France for its support during the Revolution as well to change the custom of looking backward rather than forward. The village of Calais, a few miles to Montpelier's north, was also surveyed by Davis, and one assumes its French name was derived for the same reason.

The earliest known view of Montpelier by Sarah Waltrous, 1821. It depicts the first statehouse. *VHS.*

Montpelier's charter was granted by Vermont governor Thomas Chittenden, a source of pride to the grantees who felt honored to have a title to land that was not complicated by a franchise awarded by New Hampshire or New York. In addition to Jacob Davis, notables such as Timothy Bigelow, Matthew Lyon, Joseph Fay, Moses Robinson, Ira Allen (land speculator, surveyor and brother of Ethan) and Thomas Chittenden were included among the sixty grantees. More notable inclusions were two women: Mary Galusha and Sybil Goodrich. A descendant of Colonel Bigelow offers an alternate source for the town's name—but more about that later.

In all, 23,040 acres (of indeterminate boundaries) were deeded to the proprietors with the provision that each of the named individuals was to plant five acres and build a home eighteen feet square within three years of the date on which the charter was issued. Oh yes, the pine trees suitable for a ship's mast were reserved for the state (presumably to equip a navy in this landlocked territory). A revised charter was issued in 1804 that fixed a boundary with Middlesex (yet another town with a named borrowed from Connecticut, Massachusetts and/or England) using a birch tree on the banks of the Onion River ("Onion" was a direct translation of the Abenaki-named *Winooski*). The revised charter also reserved land for a grammar school, a seminary or college and "a minister of the gospel."

In this fashion, the town was named and settled, but it was not yet the state capital. Designating Colonel Jacob Davis as Montpelier's first settler is, for some, problematic—the Abenaki plied trade routes through central Vermont for centuries—and others point to Joel Frizzle (an original proprietor), who had over one hundred acres in the southwest corner of the town conveyed to him by the proprietors of Arlington in 1786. Frizzle, it is said in Thompson's *History of Montpelier*, "felled a few trees, planted a little corn among the logs, after the Indian fashion, and erected a very small log cabin, and moved his family, himself, and his wife—a little red haired French woman—into it from Canada."

Jacob and Rebecca Davis were, however, the first to permanently settle in the town in 1787, building a log hut on the North Branch, near what is now the old county jail on lower Elm Street. He erected a more permanent structure the following year, and soon the hills and valleys around town saw Jacob Davis's surveying rod held upright by Joel Frizzle, who, upon the completion of the survey, sold his holdings and moved back to Canada. Daniel P. Thompson's 1860 book *History of Montpelier* remarked that Frizzle "could not properly be called the first settler, nor properly, indeed, any kind of settler but was one of those roving, half

Looking east, this view shows the statehouse in 1853. From *Gleason's Pictorial. PH.*

savage men who are ever to be found near the borders of civilization, and who yet ever flee before its approach."

When Colonel Davis's sons joined him in the new settlement, Jacob—the eldest son—took fishing tackle to the banks of the North Branch. Using "some raw pork for bait," according to Thompson, "with a half-bushel basket to hold the fish, he threw in towards the middle of the stream to await the result. The instant the bait struck the water, he said, the trout, in astonishing numbers, darted forward from every direction, and like a flock of hungry chickens, commenced a keen tussle for the unwonted prize thus suddenly dropped among them." After a half hour of fishing in this fashion, he had "filled his basket with trout of the weight of a half pound and upwards to two pounds."

Over the next four years, twenty families moved into town, roads were built, a mill was erected and a burgeoning town was growing apace in both the valleys and the hills. At that time, East Montpelier and Montpelier were one entity with almost simultaneous settlement. Colonel Davis's cousin Parley settled the higher ground east of Jacob's domain in what is now East Montpelier Center. Parley Davis was a highly regarded and influential officer in the local militia, eventually attaining the rank of general. Other villages that were later absorbed by town and city included Gallison Hill (where, naturally, many of the Gallison clan resided) and Gould Hill. These names are still in popular parlance. Esther Swift, in her indispensible book *Vermont Place Names*, notes: "An old Indian is given credit for the picturesque East Montpelier place-name, Horn of the Moon. It seems that he once lost his wife and later found her at the place he called 'horn of the moon.' A school at the intersection of two country roads has always been called Horn of the Moon School, and a tiny body of water up in the northwestern corner of town is known as Horn of the Moon Pond."

In the early years of Vermont, both as a republic and a state, the legislature met in various locations, divided between east and west. It even met once in Charlestown, New Hampshire. Parochial jealousies and regional suspicions were the greatest obstacles to determining a permanent home for Vermont's government, but by 1805, the unlikely choice of Montpelier was finally recommended for the official seat of government. Perhaps its newness and unfinished atmosphere made it less objectionable than other sites that came with political baggage, but more to the point, its central location and the willingness of its citizens to subsidize the building of a statehouse were the deciding factors. Early visitor and Yale professor Timothy Dwight of New Haven, Connecticut, was surprised by the decision. He records his impressions in one of his famous letters from his book *Travels in New England*:

> *Montpelier is situated at the confluence of two head waters of the Onion river. The intervals on this stream commence at its mouth; and extend, with few interruptions, to this place. The valley is here large enough to contain a village, of perhaps thirty or forty houses, within a reasonable vicinity. The hills, which are high and sudden, approach so near to the river, as to form a defile, rather than an open valley. About thirty or forty buildings; houses, stores, and shops are already erected here. A few other buildings, and among them a State House, are begun. The Legislature of Vermont has lately fixed upon this spot, as the permanent seat of government. The determination is obviously unwise; and must have resulted from very limited, or very prejudiced views. By that association of ideas, which is so prominent a characteristic of the human mind, a little town, when the seat of government, will always impart its littleness to the Legislature, and to all its coadjutors. Every thing must here exist on a very limited scale. That conversation, which in the hours of leisure, cannot fail of being resorted to as a relief from the fatigue of business, must be confined, and degrading. All busy men must have their hours of relaxation; and where refined and superior amusements cannot be obtained, will to a great extent, spend those hours in such as are trifling and contemptible. The character of a town in which a Legislature holds its sessions, will be imparted to its members; and ultimately, to its measures. If this be not good, it will be bad: if it be not honorable, it will be despicable.*
>
> *Montpelier is now so small, as scarcely to furnish either shelter, or lodging, for the Legislature of this State; and its situation is such, as to forbid the hope of any future, material enlargement. As Vermont is separated into three distinct parts; the mountains and the countries East and West of them; and as the mountains can be conveniently passed only through a few clefts; Windsor and Burlington would undoubtedly be better chosen, as alternate seats of the Government, than any other towns in the State.*

Nevertheless, a statehouse was hastily erected on State Street in 1808 by Sylvanus Baldwin, architect, contractor and builder of the first bridge across the Onion River at approximately the same location as the present Main Street bridge. The legislature convened in the new capital for the first time in that year. In 1810, Montpelier would be designated as the county seat of Washington County, which heretofore had been Jefferson County, a name to which the Federalists objected. When the Federalists were again elected to office in 1814, they immediately changed the name of the county from Jefferson to Washington. In 1836, a new statehouse, designed by Ammi Young, was constructed and, when damaged by fire, rebuilt and expanded in 1859, under the direction of architect Thomas Silloway.

In the years since 1787, more families moved to the village: Langdon, Loomis, Merrill, Hubbard and Kellogg. Their names are recognizable today on the city streets and public buildings. In 1848, by an act of the legislature, Montpelier became two towns, casting off the land to the east. Esther Swift described the division: "There was considerable bitterness among the townspeople because only the residents of Montpelier village had wanted the subdivision. What it amounted to was that Montpelier got the center of government, the best water sites, and most of the people; East Montpelier got five-sixths of the land and very little else."

The water sites for harnessing hydropower made Montpelier something of a manufacturing center in the nineteenth century. The two branches of the Winooski River (the town favored a change of name from the anglicized "Onion" in hopes that it sounded more refined) provided optimal sites for dams and water turbines. Dennis Lane's factory, the Lane Shops, on Mechanic Street was, for a time in the latter half of the nineteenth century, the largest employer in Montpelier despite the presence of two great insurance companies. There were numerous factories on the south bank of the Winooski River (then in the town of Berlin) manufacturing carriages, harnesses and furniture, and gas was manufactured from bituminous coal to light the streets and some public buildings.

An 1855 watercolor by Thomas Waterman Wood. View from his Northfield Street studio. *Wood Art Gallery.*

In 1860, Daniel P. Thompson published his great book *History of Montpelier*, and residents and scholars began creating the lore that surrounds the early days of Vermont's capital. In 1905, the "Capital Centennial" was celebrated, and revisions to Montpelier history began to contradict the accepted version of how the town got its name.

Dorman B.E. Kent, in his inimitable fashion, put it baldly in his *Annals and Antics of Earlier Montpelier*:

> *Of course, our two adjoining towns were named by some person after the two French towns, Montpellier and Calais but who was it and why? We shall never know and don't give Jacob Davis the credit because he wasn't the "author." The reason for supposing that he was comes about from the statement in Thompson's history of Montpelier written in 1859. It's a fine piece of work but 'twould have been a little more accurate in places if we could believe all we see in Daniel P. Thompson believed that all pioneer settlers were angels who wore men's pants. And he thought Jacob Davis was the Angel de Luxe.*

Descendents of Timothy Bigelow, whose name was the first on the town's charter, have asserted that it was he, a hero of the Revolutionary War, who first suggested the name. Louise Bigelow, who wrote the

Main Street, 1950s. *PH.*

historical novel *Colonel Timothy Bigelow* in 1941, asserts in the foreword to her book:

> *Congress realizing how much back pay was due Colonel Bigelow for his services, granted him twenty-three thousand forty acres of land in Vermont in lieu of money. I have heard my grandfather say that all the satisfaction Colonel Bigelow ever got from the ownership of the land was the ability to name the town, Montpelier in honor of his friend and comrade-in-arms, the Marquis de Lafayette.*

There are various problems with the Bigelow narrative, primarily the fact that the U.S. Congress, at that time, did not have the authority to make grants in the independent Republic of Vermont. And why did Bigelow suggest the name Montpelier instead of Lafayette?

Although the knowledgeable (and irascible) Dorman Kent has his fun with D.P. Thompson, there is evidence that Jacob Davis surveyed both Calais and Montpelier. Is it a coincidence that they share French names?

We very likely will never know how, exactly, Montpelier got its name, but the question is still an interesting puzzle after all these years.

Chester Wright

Montpelier's First Minister Describes the Moral Climate of the Early Days

Chester Wright found the denizens of Vermont's capital city to have wandered as far from the path of righteousness as one could imagine. In 1808, he had come to Montpelier by way of Dartmouth and Yale Divinity School to be settled as Montpelier's first minister. To grateful acclaim, he oversaw the "religious revival" of a town whose "streets echoed with ribaldry and profaneness." He was revered as a village elder until he ran afoul of the local fraternal order and was summarily dismissed in December 1830.

The Great Awakening had ensured that a pronounced Christian influence permeated most regions of America, and Vermont was no exception. As Montpelier's historian D.P. Thompson noted, when a "moral Hercules" was needed to grapple with the town's

Chester Wright, Congregationalist minister. *VHS*.

"moral deformities," the new state capital was fortunate to acquire the services of Chester Wright.

Montpelier's first settlers arrived in 1787, and by 1800, the population had swelled to 890. Reverend Wright described the situation in a report for the *Vermont Evangelical Magazine* of 1811:

> *The first settlers not being disposed to encourage an attention to religious concerns, no religious order was observed in the place for a number of years. The inhabitants, as might be expected, became generally dissipated, and a deplorable state of morals was the result. The Sabbath, instead of being observed as the day of holy rest, was improved as a season of relaxation from ordinary business, only for purpose of amusement, convivial entertainments at public houses, or shops, sleigh-riding, trading, or gambling; and the language of profanity was the common dialect.*

Wright noted that there had seldom been any preaching in town, but nevertheless, a group of Congregationalists petitioned the legislature to recognize their local society and cast about for a minister. In February 1808, Reverend Wright was asked to preach a few sermons—the first pulpit was a temporary venue in the new statehouse—and, being found satisfactory, was invited to assume the duties of Congregational minister. This first minister in Montpelier "was engaged on trial for 12 months and at the end of the year was made the settled pastor at a salary of $50 for the first year, $375 for the second, and after that $400 with the use of a convenient parsonage." His home at 159 State Street still stands, a handsome Federal-style structure erected in 1808. Today, it houses the offices of one of Montpelier's premier legal practices.

Chester Wright was born in Hanover, New Hampshire, in 1776. His father was a farmer, and his mother, as noted in Wright's obituary, was an "excellent and pious woman." Wright expected to follow his father's path, purchasing a farm in Berkshire, Vermont, at the age of twenty-one. But heeding the "Lord, who called him out of darkness into this marvelous light, he immediately quit his occupation, disposed of his worldly goods, and land and the implements of husbandry; to prepare to preach the gospel." He attended Middlebury College and was graduated in 1806, studied theology with Dr. Burton of Thetford and finished his course of study with Dr. Timothy Dwight of New Haven, Connecticut. The Yale theologian had famously visited Montpelier some years earlier and found it a cultural and economic backwater, hardly fit for a state capital.

Chester Wright House, lower State Street. *PH.*

Wright was eager to rise to the challenge he found in Montpelier. "Here," he wrote, "was a good field for ministerial labor." His flock, initially, was small—just seventeen members. But by the time of his ordination a year later, it had grown to twenty-nine.

John Gridley's 1842 book *History of Montpelier* records an early religious experience under Wright's ministry. In 1810, two young ladies made a public declaration "of what they hoped the Lord in mercy had done for their souls, and freely confessed their wickedness in having hitherto rejected the offers of the gospel, and passed their days in vanity. They affectionately warned their young companions not to do as they had done, assuring them that all the gay amusements of youth were vanity and vexation of spirits."

Wright observed the impact this had on the congregation: "Many were affected, and expressed their emotions in floods of tears. On the next Lord's day, the assembly was larger than ever before known on a like occasion."

The Sunday services in those days were in two parts, one in the morning and the second part at five o'clock in the afternoon. During the intermission, news arrived of the death of a young man in Moretown, who until recently had been a resident of Montpelier. "Its effect was like the shock of an earthquake. Wild consternation appeared in the eyes of members, while from others tears copiously flowed." Amid this tumult a young man arose to address the assembly:

> *He confessed his sins in the most feeling manner, and especially his opposition to the preached gospel, begged forgiveness of the preacher, and of all present informed that he, with another young man whose mind was equally affected, had spent a considerable part of the preceding day in a retired place, in reading and in prayer—spoke largely of his former wickedness and obstinacy in rejecting Christ, entreated all the youth present to come to Jesus.*

In Gridley's account, Reverend Wright noted that the town was subdued the following day. Instead of "the usual noise and bustle, this place was as still as a Sabbath." On Tuesday, a religious meeting held at the statehouse was very well attended, and Wright observed that "many were pricked in the heart." The religious fervor continued unabated for several days with public professions of conviction among Montpelier's youth. Membership in the Congregational Church steadily increased to seventy in a few months' time, with the greatest share between the ages of eighteen and twenty-four. The first Congregational church was built of brick in 1820 on the site of Bethany Church. Before that, services were usually held in the statehouse.

By all measures, Wright's early tenure as Montpelier's first minister appeared to be successful. He soon married Charlotte Whitney of Royalton and raised a family. A son, James, would become a Universalist minister. In 1813, a disastrous fire destroyed the cotton mill in town. As citizens rushed to put out the flames, they saw their "small, spare" pastor, according to D.P. Thompson's *History of Montpelier*, "standing on the reach-pole of a rear endangered building, dripping with water, handling buckets, and with the voice and energy of a young lion, giving orders to the crowd below." His son, James, would execute strikingly similar services in Montpelier's great fire of 1875.

In July 1828, Chester performed the marriage rites of one of Montpelier's most famous and important citizens. J.P Miller, a stern abolitionist and hero of the Greek war for independence, was known as the "American Daredevil." In Greece, he had been awarded the sword of the late Lord Byron for his bravery in battle. The same sword is currently on display at the Vermont History Center in Barre.

In succeeding years, Wright would incite Miller's ire by his advocacy of the American Colonization Society, a group that was at odds with abolitionists because they proposed returning slaves to Africa, primarily to the new state of Liberia. In this position, Wright was supported by Timothy Hubbard, one of the earliest settlers of Montpelier. The two factions almost came to blows in 1835, when nationally known abolitionist and Unitarian minister Samuel May spoke from the pulpit of the Congregational church.

Right: J.P. Miller, the "American Daredevil." *VHS*.

Below: "The Old Brick Church." The first Congregational church on the site of what is now Bethany Church. *VHS*.

Wright eventually became a lightning rod for abolitionist anger, reviled in the pages of William Lloyd Garrison's *Liberator*. He sparred in print with editors of the Boston paper and very likely alienated proponents of the abolitionist cause in Montpelier.

Other views, however, strained the pastor's relationship with his congregation and led to his dismissal. D.P. Thompson, in his *History of Montpelier*, asked, "Why was he dismissed in his old age, and, with broken health compelled to go abroad or starve?"

The 1826 murder of William Morgan in Batavia, New York, incited a spate of anti-Masonic fervor throughout the country. Morgan, it was said, intended to reveal secrets of the fraternal order and was violently silenced. Wright embraced the ensuing anti-Masonic cause, lending his name and office to the movement. His dismissal in 1830, wrote Thompson, "grew out of the agitation then going on respecting the merits and demerits of the Masonic Institution, to which many of his people, and quite a number of the leading members of his church, belonged. It was claimed by friends of that order that Mr. Wright had been found to entertain opinions adverse to the institution and that he persisted in openly expressing them."

Eventually, Reverend Wright found another parish in Hardwick, where, again, he was the object of national speculation when he took on the new charismatic movement in town. They called themselves the New Lights but were referred to in the press as Holy Rollers because of their practice of falling to the floor of the church and rolling about in paroxysms of religious ecstasy. One newspaper account described their practice: "They began a mission of disturbing religious meetings by screams and yells, pretending that they were acting under the power of the Spirit. They got possession of a meeting house in Hardwick and held service there, barking like dogs and imitating the noises of beasts. But their chief worship was rolling on the floor, and they got the name of 'holy rollers.'"

Reverend Wright noted that it began in 1837 at the South Meetinghouse in Hardwick, and on numerous occasions, ministers were silenced by "tumultuous noises." It happened to Wright once, and in response, he prepared a powerful sermon, "The Devil in the Nineteenth Century," which he delivered at the church on May 6, 1838. Wright's work is a fine example of deductive reasoning in which he demonstrates that the obstreperous members of the church were either willfully or unwittingly deluded into performing the services of Satan. When he preached the sermon, the New Lights attempted to silence him with their howls, but he had arranged for a constable to remove them. Wright was able to convey the complete text of his sermon, and the disruptions ceased.

For the vanquished pastor, this was a final triumph before his return to Montpelier to live the remainder of his life. He passed away in 1840 in the town that had once spurned him, but in his passing, historian D.P. Thompson noted:

> *While he knew of a wrong, a vice or injurious habit among any of his people, he gave himself no rest till he saw the wrong righted, the vice overcome and the habit corrected. He was everywhere found exhorting men individually as well as collectively. Though often rebuffed, he was never discouraged, but persistently returned again and again to the work of accomplishing his object, till even the most obdurate began to look upon it as a matter of course that they must hear from their misdeeds and delinquencies, and at length to consider that the cheapest thing to be done, was to reform themselves.*

Common Crackers

The Famous Vermont Common Cracker's Origins in Montpelier

A gaggle of local sports was gathered around the cracker barrel at the general store in Walden, Vermont, a few generations ago. Between the spitting and chewing and eating the occasional cracker crowned with a thin slice of cheddar cut from a wheel under a glass dome, they were marveling at the newest item just stocked in the rural emporium: a bunch of bananas. It was the first time the tropical fruit had been seen there, and when know-it-all Elmer Davis joined the throng, the men looked sideways at one another, as if they had a secret. Storekeeper Hiram Wheeler held one up and said, "Elmer, do you like bananas?" Davis nodded in assent. "Well then, have this one," said the storekeeper.

"Don't mind if I do," he replied, stuffing one end in his mouth and biting hard through the peel. As the boys struggled with laughter, Hiram counseled, "When they're tough, Elmer, sometimes we peels 'em." With that, the sports collapsed with laughter, and Elmer choked down the fruit and beat a hasty retreat.

It is hard to imagine the country store without its cracker barrel and the attendant throng gathered to sample the generally free biscuits as hard as flint and so mildly flavored as to be essentially tasteless. In Montpelier, we called them Cross Crackers. Elsewhere, they were called Montpelier Crackers, and they were produced in a legendary Montpelier bakery that had been in existence on Main Street for over one hundred years, having been established in 1828. It is even harder to imagine that such a bland item could have sustained a major industry in central Vermont until one

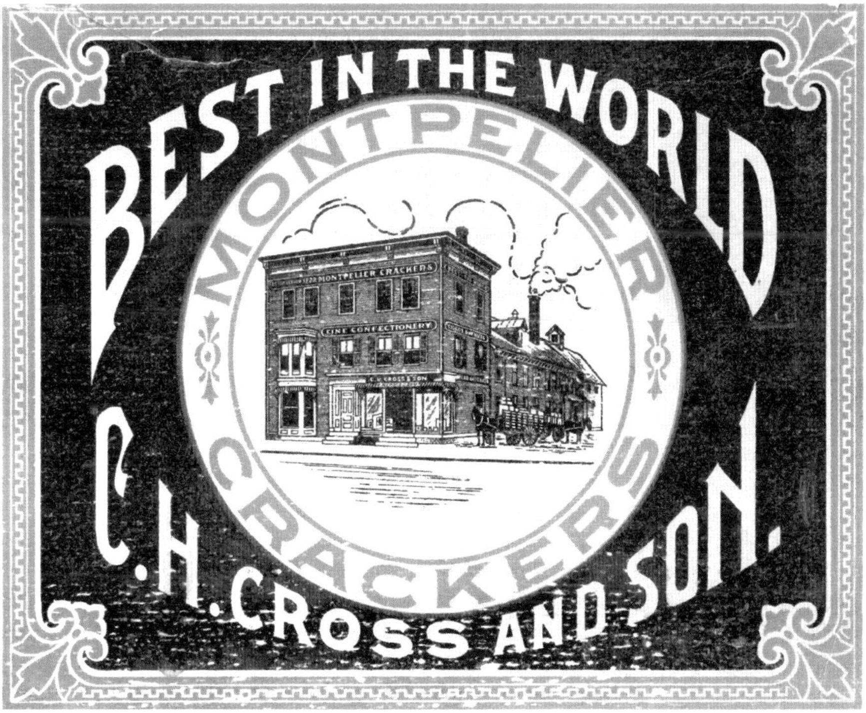

Cross Cracker logo: "Best in the World." *VHS.*

remembers that these crackers were only intended to be a vehicle to support the enjoyment of something else, such as cheese, oyster stew or raspberry jam or just to add substance to a bowl of milk.

The Cross company made the crackers available by the barrel for $2.60. That price, in 1908, would buy a storekeeper approximately 1,200 crackers, according to L.F. Willard in a 1981 article in *Yankee* magazine. By 1942, Willard wrote, "you could still buy a barrel of crackers from the Cross Baking Company, but the price had risen to $6.30, plus .35 for the barrel." By that measure, a storekeeper might be reviled as stingy if he did not leave the top off the barrel.

Weston Cate, lifelong central Vermont resident and former head of the Vermont Historical Society, recalled in 1981 that "at the height of it operations the firm did six million dollars worth of business annually and employed 160 men and women." Although the crackers may have been the most famous edible produced in the capital city, the Cross Bakery also produced thirty thousand loaves of bread every day. So essential to the welfare of Montpelier was its production of baked goods that, in the aftermath of the 1927 flood, an emergency airlift dropped live yeast on a Towne Hill farm clearing, in order that the baking of bread could resume to help feed the hungry residents isolated by the raging torrent.

The family patriarch, Timothy Cross, began business on the site now occupied by Montpelier's Bethany Church. He had lived near the shores of Lake Winnipesaukee before coming to Montpelier in 1828. Timothy hired his younger brother Charles as an apprentice for three years in exchange for meals and clothing. Brother Charles was the inspiration behind the cracker, inventing a baked product that could be wholesaled to general stores and had a shelf life that could be measured in months, if not years. Despite this success, Charles left his brother's bakery for a few years to run a grocery store. "I did not sell rum," he proudly declared. However, in 1843, he rejoined his brother's business to concentrate his energies on their most well-known product. The crackers were so popular that Charles soon bought out his brother.

A historian for the New England Historical Society traces the origins of Cross's crackers to hard tack:

> *Soldiers, sailors, explorers and travelers have carried some variation of cracker with them for centuries. Hard tack is simply an unleavened water and flour cracker that has been baked to within an inch of its life. It will last virtually forever (hard tack produced for the War of 1812 was stored and then brought out for use in the Civil War, for example, none the worse for wear). But hard tack soon gave rise (forgive the pun) to more elegant crackers for domestic use. The addition of yeast, a rising period of 24 hours and a long period of kneading, followed by baking and drying, resulted in a puffy white cracker with a hard thick outer shell—the common cracker.*

Weston Cate noted, "Charles Cross started in a modest way but on a definite schedule. Three days a week he mixed and baked his crackers. On alternate days he hitched up his horse and peddled his crackers from door to door." The horse, by the way, was put to good use on baking days, turning the special stone oven that, according to Willard's article in *Yankee*, "was rotated by means of a horse that walked in a circle. Charles had an alternating schedule: he used the horse in the bakery one day, and the next day hitched it to a wagon to deliver the crackers." The horse was hitched to a sweep to move the soapstone shelf that held the cracker baking tins. The Cross Bakery continued to use horses for local delivery of the crackers until after the great flood of 1927.

Charles H. Cross was born in Sanbornton, New Hampshire, in 1812. It was said that when he came to Montpelier to join his brother's baking business, he had just four cents in his pocket. At that time, the crackers were made by hand, a tedious endeavor. The 1893 *Montpelier Souvenir* recalled:

> *He bought an old meat cart and fitted it up as a baker's wagon, and made crackers with his own hands and peddled them in his cart. About a year later his business had increased so that he was enabled to put in another room and another oven. By this time he had some help from his sons. He continued in this manner about a year when he went into partnership with his brother Timothy and they enlarged the business by hiring a larger building and putting in two ovens. Two years later, Timothy retired from the concern, and Charles bought a cracker machine, which revolutionized the business, and did away with the work by hand. His trade increased very rapidly, until he had two double teams, and hired six men. These teams went out from Montpelier in all directions, from 30 to 80 miles. In 1856 he bought the old Masonic Hall, moved in, enlarged the facilities, and put in three tile ovens. The business continued in this way until 1863, when his son L. Bart Cross was taken into partnership, and the firm was much the gainer by this infusion of new blood. In 1867 they sold their building (the old Masonic Hall) to the Congregational Church, and bought, very near their old location, a lot which was 50 feet fronting on Main Street and extending back 375 feet. Here they put in a rotary oven, and fitted up the premises with all the machinery that modern ingenuity had invented for the prosecution of their work.*

Their up-to-date machinery still included a horse-powered oven—this time using a treadmill. In 1897, it was reported that the Main Street bakery produced over fifty thousand crackers a day. An 1891 report on the industries

L. Bart Cross. *VHS*.

of Vermont observed, "They own and occupy a series of five buildings in their business and give constant employment to a large force of skilled hands."

Child's *Gazetteer of Washington County* (1889) remarked:

> *Mr. Cross in all these years spared no pains or expense in producing the best goods possible, and labors with the ready cooperation of his son to give his very numerous customers an equivalent dollar for dollar. And the result is the "Montpelier Cracker"' and the other productions from C.H. Cross & Sons bakery have a reputation unequalled by any other establishment in New England. Mr. Cross has also found time, notwithstanding his close attention to his constantly increasing business, to aid in building up the town, and it is generally reported that he has built more residences than any other citizen of the place.*

Cross was a member of the Republican Party and a devoted Methodist. When a new seminary was proposed for Montpelier, he joined the board of trustees and could be counted on for financial support for the fledgling institution that was to become Vermont College and later the Vermont College of Fine Arts. Cross married Caroline Houston of Enfield, New Hampshire, and their son, L. Bart Cross, took the reins of the bakery upon the demise of his father. When Charles Cross died in 1905 at the age of ninety-three, he was the oldest man in Montpelier and the oldest baker in New England.

The younger Cross operated the bakery for three years and then sold the firm to George L. Edson, who was a direct descendent of Colonel Jacob Davis, Montpelier's first settler. George was eventually joined in the enterprise by his son, G. Lansdale Edson. In all the years the company was in operation in Montpelier, it had just five leaders from two families, and at that time, it was considered to be the oldest commercial firm operating in the state.

In 1927, a flood of biblical proportions ravaged Vermont. Central Vermont was especially hard hit, and Montpelier was no exception. At the Cross Bakery, floodwaters rendered all but one oven inoperable. An electric oven on the second floor was discovered to be functional, and a storeroom on the second floor contained flour and some other supplies that remained unharmed by the rising waters. When airplanes began dropping emergency supplies on an airstrip on Towne Hill, a relief agency asked if bread was needed. "Send us the yeast and we will make the bread," was the immediate reply, wired in response. The *Argus* reported, "For the duration of the emergency the relief planes dropped containers of bakers yeast to the field and the bakers continued to keep the electric oven busy twenty-four hours a day."

Lansdale Edson was regarded as a munificent corporate officer and was, reported the *Argus*, "called Lansdale by his employees and prefers it that way. He takes pride in the long-standing reputation of the company for quality and service but dislikes personal acclaim." The newspaper described the progressive benefits enjoyed by the employees of the firm, including various forms of insurance, as well as a "group annuity retirement system. The Cross Company is believed to be the first baking company in New England to install such a complete program of protection for its employees and is one of the first in the country. Still attached to the bakery building are the gold-leafed signs that acclaim to all, as they have for so many years: 'Established 1828—Montpelier Crackers—Best in the World.'"

That report, published in 1945, did not consider how difficult the years of World War II were for the company. Even though it added a variety of other products to its inventory, the business struggled until, with the loss of a major contract, it closed its Montpelier factory and, in 1959, consolidated operations in Claremont, New Hampshire. Finally, in 1966,

The Cross Baking Company adjacent to Bethany Church on Main Street. *VHS.*

its manufacturing facility was closed there, as well. As the company went into receivership, the assets were sold to settle its debt, and Vrest Orton of the iconic Vermont Country Store bought the cracker-making equipment. He invited Lansdale Edson to supervise the installation of the equipment, and the famous Montpelier Crackers took a new lease on life. Now called Vermont Common Crackers, the Vermont Country Store continues to bake them at its bakery in North Clarendon.

Generations of Montpelierites remember the wood-frame Italianate building at 101 Main Street that was headquarters for the baking company. In later years, the space was occupied by a pastry and penny candy shop. The edifice was originally constructed in the years after the Civil War and expanded as required by a thriving business. On Christmas Eve 1980, the landmark Cross Building was destroyed by a disastrous fire in the heart of downtown Montpelier. The former site of the bakery is now occupied by City Center.

Sam Upham

Civil War Counterfeiter

Samuel Upham, it was said during the Civil War, had done more to thwart the Confederate cause than George McClellan, general of the Army of the Potomac. And Upham, it should be remembered, never served in uniform in the War of the Rebellion. His fame (and fortune) came from counterfeiting Confederate banknotes and postage stamps. He often bragged that the Southern cause had put a price of $10,000 on his head, so damaging to the Southern economy were his forgeries. As will be seen, Upham was a patriot by happenstance, not intent.

Samuel Curtis Upham was a native of Montpelier, Vermont, having been born into a farm family in 1819. His parents, Samuel and Sally, have been described as "zealous Methodists." His uncle William Upham was among the early settlers of Montpelier, having arrived in 1802. William eventually represented Vermont in the United States Senate, counting Daniel Webster among his friends.

Samuel Upham's colorful career incorporated a stint in the navy, a trip to the California gold fields in 1849 and fame as a songwriter and poet. At other times, he wrote for newspapers and published travelogues such as *Notes of a Voyage to California via Cape Horn*. The 1878 account offers insights to the early history of Sacramento and dismisses romantic notions of ocean travel. "Descriptions of a life on the ocean wave read very prettily on shore, but the *reality* of a sea voyage speedily dispels the romance." At one point, he remarks that a mountainous visage seen from the coast of Brazil "recalled vividly to mind recollections of my boyhood home in consequence of its resemblance to Camel's Hump."

Camel's Hump. *VHS.*

The limitations of Vermont's rustic capital were too confining for an adventurer like Samuel Curtis Upham. The prosaic life of his father, a blacksmith and farmer, was not to the liking of young Samuel (the fifth in a row so named), and he fled Montpelier at age twenty to seek his fortune. His destination was New York City, as far culturally from Montpelier, Vermont, as any place in the young republic. Ben Tarnoff wrote in *Moneymakers*, "For a young man from the countryside, New York would be a fast education. It certainly offered more opportunities for youthful indiscretion than Montpelier: saloons, opium dens, and brothels, to name a few." Upham became a bookkeeper in the city's commercial district but soon gave in to wanderlust and joined the navy in 1842. He served on cruises to Constantinople and the Gulf of Mexico. Upon discharge, he returned to Montpelier. The attraction of urban life soon drew him to Philadelphia, where he found employment as an accountant for a lumber company. He married, sired a daughter and then heard some remarkable news. Gold had been discovered at Sutter's Mill in California.

In spite of the needs of his young family, Upham could not forsake the allure of easy money and adventure on the other side of the continent. In January 1849, he set sail for San Francisco by way of Cape Horn, the opening of the Panama Canal being over fifty years in the future. In his diary, Upham wrote, "Having been a rolling stone all my life, consequently

Samuel Curtis Upham—counterfeiter. *PH.*

have gathered no moss. And now in search of 'the golden fleece,' and may return shorn." The shipboard experience was unforgettable with long periods of tedium interspersed with drunken revels, gambling and fistfights. The ship reached San Francisco in August, after a voyage of seven months. Upham's account of the gold rush and early San Francisco is fascinating. He found prospecting a more physically challenging ordeal than he had anticipated and, after some success panning for gold, abandoned it for mercantile pursuits in San Francisco, a city experiencing a boom in almost every respect. He eventually found work as a bookkeeper for the town's first newspaper. Aspiring to greater journalistic ambitions, he accepted an offer to help publish a newspaper in Sacramento. In addition to managing the paper's finances, he was also the reporter for hometown news. Almost before his eyes, he witnessed the beginnings of a great California city.

Regretfully, in the fall of 1850, he felt obliged to return to Philadelphia, to the responsibilities of a wife and daughter. After returning home, he expanded his family with two sons and, with the confidence gained from his experience in Sacramento, started a weekly newspaper, the *Sunday Mercury*.

The *Mercury* provided weekend entertainment for Philadelphia's middle class during the years leading up to the Civil War. With the assault on Fort Sumter, an anti-Southern sentiment prevailed in the City of Brotherly Love, and as the cause of secession flourished below the Mason-Dixon line, new sensibilities became manifest. The Confederate states, struggling to finance a war, started printing their own currency, a phenomenon that aroused great curiosity in the North.

Upham found the fascination with Confederate banknotes to be a compelling opportunity. He noticed that in 1862, when the *Philadelphia Inquirer* printed a facsimile of the five-dollar note in the newspaper, the print run of that issue sold out immediately. He had the idea of printing some bank notes as novelties and selling them from a stationery store he had opened on Chestnut Street.

Making his way to the offices of the *Inquirer*, he persuaded them to sell him the printing block for the notes. He added a small print line in the bottom margin: "FACSIMILE OF A TREASURY NOTE LATELY ISSUED BY THE CONFEDERATE GOVERNMENT; RICHMOND, VA" and advertised the facsimiles for sale in early March. The response was astonishing. His initial print run of 3,000 $5 notes sold quickly at a penny apiece. As buyers learned that the facsimile line could easily be trimmed from the banknotes, sales skyrocketed. Soon, the stationery store was selling more currency than anything else, and Upham became, to his delight, an inadvertent counterfeiter. He received bulk orders

Upham's five-dollar CSA counterfeit. *George Tremmel.*

for his currency from Yankee traders who purchased goods such as cotton in the South with Upham's counterfeits. He soon expanded his market by purchasing full-page ads in various Union publications offering various denominations of currency. One flier indicated that he had sold 500,000 facsimiles in the previous ninety days. For the discounted price of fifty cents (plus eighteen cents postage) one could order 100 "banknotes" through the mail. Another advertisement offered $20,000 worth of Confederate "notes" for only $5 in Union currency.

The Richmond, Virginia *Daily Dispatch* complained bitterly about the false banknotes, observing that they were so expertly printed there was no way of telling them from the originals. In fact, when offered a choice between Upham's currency and the real thing, most people chose the fakes—they were better executed than the originals.

As Union soldiers made their way south, they often passed through Philadelphia, stopping at Upham's Chestnut Street store to fill their pockets and rucksacks with the false banknotes. A Southern newspaper noted that the Union soldiers were "fortified with exhaustless quantities of Philadelphia Confederate notes which they used to buy everything from horses to sugar to tobacco." It should come as no surprise that the U.S. government turned a blind eye to Upham's activities. Its logic was that the Rebel government was illegal and so was its currency. In effect, no law could be broken by counterfeiting the illegal tender.

Union officer Chester Barney wrote of the phenomenon when he commanded Iowa troops in Arkansas:

> *It was here that I learned that many of our men had commenced a large business in Confederate currency, or what seemed just as good, the facsimile money, which was deemed by the rebel sympathizers better and safer than greenbacks. Having learned of this weakness of our "Southern brethren" before leaving Rolla* [Missouri], *many of them had brought large amounts of this spurious cash which only purported to be an imitation of the Confederate note, and were now passing it off freely in the way of trade, but always in such amounts as required at least some change in return. We met here many who were willing to exchange "Lincoln Greenbacks" for this facsimile stuff, dollar for dollar and as the boys purchased it at Rolla for about the original cost of the paper, they made quite a handsome profit in this transaction. The Bank of Facsimile will have a large run if it redeems all its notes our boys have put in circulation in Missouri and Arkansas.*

In late May 1862, the Richmond, Virginia *Daily Dispatch* evinced its outrage at the insult to Confederate currency:

> *The Yankee swindle before us is an engraved note and so like the original, which is lithographed, that it can only be detected by the words, in very small print under the border line, "Facsimile—Sold wholesale and retail by S.C. Upham 408 Chestnut Street, Philadelphia." Who is this man Upham? A knave, swindler, and forger of the most depraved and despicable sort.*
>
> *Doubtless the counterfeits in question have been scattered wherever an execrable Yankee soldier polluted the soil with his cloven foot.*

Shortly thereafter, in the Confederate states, the manufacture of counterfeit notes was made a crime punishable by death.

Ben Tarnoff's *Moneymakers* suggested that the Upham notes were so successful that printers in New York and other Northern cities were making cheap knockoffs of his fake currency. "Beware of Base Imitations!" he announced in his May flyer. "Each and every facsimile issued by me bears my imprint." Tarnoff elaborates on the flaw in Upham's business strategy: "The more counterfeits he sold, the less valuable Confederate notes became, depressing the demand for his product. His fortunes were tied to those of the Confederacy, a peculiar situation for a Northern patriot." In the spring of 1863, in the face of dwindling demand, he stopped printing the Confederate bills.

Upham closed his Chestnut Street shop and opened a new enterprise less than a mile away. He now devoted his energies to making patent medicine, which he advertised with the warning, "Beware of Counterfeits." Ben

Tarnoff's *Moneymakers* notes, "Upham moved from one scheme to another, from counterfeiting to quackery. He had nothing to recommend him but his talent as a salesman, which was considerable. His business thrived."

In later years, Upham turned to writing wistful patriotic ballads celebrating the history he saw being made during the California gold rush. Tarnoff wrote, "Sixty-six years old, he died neither rich nor poor but somewhere in between. His brief obituary in the *Philadelphia Inquirer* didn't include a single word about his moneymaking career" but noted that he "was a poet and a prolific writer of songs." He had lived the last four years of his life on the Gulf Coast of Florida.

Suffering from stomach cancer, he died at home.

Daniel Pierce Thompson

Montpelier's First Historian and Great Eccentric

When he is remembered at all, Daniel Pierce Thompson is usually known as the author of *The Green Mountain Boys*, a romantic account of the era of the Revolutionary War when "Yorkers" battled New Hampshire partisans for title to Vermont, and Ethan Allen engineered a military triumph at Fort Ticonderoga. The book has been in print almost continually since its first appearance in 1839. In Montpelier, however, Thompson is also known as the author of the essential history of the Capital City: *History of the Town of Montpelier; from the Time It Was First Chartered in 1781 to the Year 1860*. This great history of Montpelier was published in 1860 and has never been supplanted. Thompson had an advantage over all subsequent historians—he knew the founders personally and collected their stories as earnestly and frequently as he rambled the banks of the Winooski River with his fishing pole.

Daniel was born in Charlestown, Massachusetts, in 1795 from forebears who were among the early settlers of the Bay Colony and fought for independence in the Revolutionary War. His grandfather was killed at the Battle of Lexington.

When he was just five years old, his family moved from Charlestown to a farm in Berlin, Vermont, that abutted the town line of Montpelier. A granite marker honors the Thompson family farm, indicating the roadside where the Thompson homestead was originally located (near the present site of Cody Chevrolet). Their property was bisected by the Stevens Branch of the Winooski River, and in his *History of the Town of Montpelier*, Thompson

The 1929 dedication of a marker designating the boyhood home of D.P. Thompson. Dorman Kent is on the far right. *VHS.*

records the naming of the branch with a historical account in which the author plays a small part:

> *A reputable young man by the name of Stevens, residing in Corinth, when that was a frontier town was engaged to a girl of the same town, who, from fickleness or some unwarranted freak of jealousy, broke her plighted faith, and suddenly married another.*
>
> *This so wrought on the mind and feelings of Stevens that he soon resolved to banish himself from society into the lone forests, never to return. He provided himself with guns, traps, and other things composing the hunter's outfit, and having made his way to the bank of the stream that subsequently took his name, about a quarter of a mile from its mouth, on the farm occupied, for the first forty years of the present century, by Daniel Thompson, the father of the writer of these pages. This was in early autumn; and nothing more was heard from him until the following spring, when two hunters, passing that way, found his dead body near his camp. He had evidently been seized with sickness, induced by despondency, had breathed his last alone in the dark wilderness. The exact spot where*

Historic marker for Daniel Pierce Thompson's boyhood home. *PH.*

> *the hunters had buried him was not known till about the year 1806, when Mr. Thompson, in plowing up a spot from which he had removed an old hedge fence, turned out his bones. I, then a small boy, was present on that occasion, and the sight of these remains as they were thrown out by the deep furrow that was made lengthwise through them, with the rust-eaten jack-knife lying in the midst, caused it to become one of the most vivid of my early recollections, and subsequently led me to make minute inquiries of the oldest settlers in all that related to the unfortunate hunter.*

Thompson's early years were consumed with the practical activities associated with claiming a homestead from the wilderness. He learned to fish and hunt, paddle a boat and plant and hoe as he acquired the skills of a Vermont farm boy. We know from his autobiographical novel *Locke Amsden* that he hated farming and used all his resources to find an alternative way to make a living.

Amazingly, he never entered the town of Montpelier until he was twelve years old. The occasion was a Fourth of July celebration in 1807 on the new statehouse grounds. When Thompson and his brother Joseph reached the foundation of the soon-to-be-constructed statehouse, they saw stakes marking out the street that would lead to the capitol building. The boys joined the throng assembled to listen to the Independence Day proclamation, and Thompson heard the first oration of his life. His biographer, John Flitcroft, noted that in exactly twenty years Thompson would himself mount the stage to deliver the annual Fourth of July address.

At about the same time, Thompson noted the construction of the Pavilion House, the first iteration of a hotel that was to stand in the same location near the statehouse until it was razed in 1970. The original Pavilion was designed by Sylvanus Baldwin, the self-taught architect who planned the first statehouse. The present Pavilion reopened in 1971 as a state building with an office for the governor and facilities for the Vermont Historical Society. The mansard-roofed replica pays homage to the well-known version of the hotel that opened in 1876 and incorporates some of its original components in its reconstruction.

Thompson regularly attended ceremonial functions in Montpelier, which became more frequent with the completion of the statehouse in 1808. Schooling for Daniel amounted to irregular attendance at the district school and what lessons his parents were able to impart. The chance acquisition of a volume of English poetry awakened his thirst for learning. With money earned from a small flock of sheep and skins from a trap line, he was able to purchase a Latin grammar book, a volume of Virgil and a text on arithmetic. He spent a winter boarding with a clergyman with the intent of "fitting for college." Eventually, he was admitted to Middlebury College, which in 1817 had been in existence for less than twenty years.

He completed his course of study in 1820 and briefly served as a tutor for a wealthy family in Virginia. The position is remarkable for the opportunity it allowed the young man to interview Thomas Jefferson at Monticello. Thompson's notes on the occasion indicate that they discussed Patrick Henry, slavery and Jefferson's plans for the University of Virginia. Thompson spent more than three years in Virginia and studied law when not engaged in tutoring his pupil.

By the time he returned to Montpelier in 1824, he was ready to open a law office but instead found related employment in official capacities such as judge of the probate court and as a legislative assistant. He was remembered as a man with varied interests, including folklore, botany and local history. His biographer noted, "His favorite recreation was fishing. Local tradition represents him as wandering through the country with his fishing rod, and stopping to chat with some old settler by the roadside or at a farmhouse door, where he would spend hours listening to reminiscences of the early settlement of Vermont."

Shortly after his return to Vermont, he was asked by Zadock Thompson (no relation) to compose a narrative sketch of Montpelier for the new *Gazetteer* he was preparing. Daniel began his research by interviewing the early settlers who still lived in town. He noted in his preface to his full-length *History of Montpelier*, "We visited, for the purpose of collecting materials for that task, the most intelligent survivors of the first settlers of Montpelier and the neighboring towns, and made minutes of the facts and incidents which we condensed into the brief sketch of the town that appears in the *Gazetteer*."

His work on the *Gazetteer* proved instrumental in preparing Thompson for undertaking a more fulsome treatment of the history of the capital city. The fact that he was often present at important events added a sense of immediacy to the work as well as a charming perspective on the city's history. As a teenager, he was in the front row of the audience when the country's participation in the War of 1812 was hotly debated between the Democrats and the Federalists on a cold February afternoon.

> *When the day arrived, we mustered out a few boys of the neighborhood, and with them proceeded on foot, to the scene of the action. As we neared the village we found every road almost literally black with the throngs of men and boys on foot, on horseback, in cutters and thickly packed double sleighs, all pouring into town and hurrying forward to the place of the appointed meeting. On reaching the State House we found the doors just being thrown open; and, standing amidst the waiting and impatient crowd, we were borne on, in the mighty rush through the principal entrance, till we were forced up close to the broad plank platform, that had been erected over the clerk's desk for the accommodation of the opposing speakers; for it was understood, that even here, the Federalists would appear in force, to prevent the passage of any resolves going to encourage the threatened war by Congress.*

It has always been a privilege to live close to government, especially for a teenager, and find oneself at hand when important ideas are debated. Daniel Thompson had found his calling—to be a witness to portentous events. Thompson recalls how Chester Wright, a beloved Montpelier clergyman, was asked to offer a benediction before the debate and how his refusal "on account of conscientious scruples about the war" was received with "a low burst of indignation." The intrusion of his personal observations allows Thompson to make much more of his town history than he otherwise would have. His history is almost as much memoir as dispassionate narrative and is more pleasurable reading as a result.

Almost one half of his history is given to biographies of influential citizens such as first settlers Colonel Jacob and Rebecca Davis, printer and publisher General Ezekiel Walton, General Parley Davis, Reverend Chester Wright, Colonel J.P. Miller and Timothy Hubbard. Many of the biographical subjects would play an important role in the history of Vermont as well as Montpelier, and many of their names will always be associated with the town. The citizens of Montpelier heartily endorsed Thompson's research and writing. In fact, at Montpelier's 1859 town meeting, he was appointed the municipality's "Official Historian," and the following year saw the publication of his magnum opus. Despite the accolade, he was often seen dressed shabbily. Historian Charles Morrissey described his demeanor: "He always looked as though he needed a haircut, walking through the village, a wooden fishing pole over his shoulder, a single suspender holding up his overalls, a broad-brimmed straw hat on his head to shield out the summer sun. He often seemed to be lost in abstractions, plodding with a preoccupied expression down the middle of the road."

In 1838, he joined Henry Stevens and two other antiquarians in forming the Vermont Historical Society. Its collections were housed at Stevens's home in Barnet until accommodation could be made in the statehouse. Thompson is remembered with a brass plaque that still hangs near the Senate chamber.

Both Thompson and Henry Stevens were recalled in Weston Cate's book about the Vermont Historical Society.

Daniel Pierce Thompson, author of *The Green Mountain Boys*. *VHS*.

> *Henry Stevens and D.P. Thompson were the state's two leading antiquarians during the middle nineteenth century. Both were named in the Society's original charter and both became Society officers.*
>
> *Both men were in love with the past, but their approaches to history were quite different. Stevens was basically a collector of manuscripts, documents, books, and historical ephemera. Thompson was an early exponent of oral history. He loved to roam the hills and valleys of the state with a fish pole over one shoulder and a pocket notebook in which he would carefully record his conversations with rural folks, especially those who could recall Revolutionary and early settlement days. Thompson, though a lawyer by profession and a writer by avocation, edited the* Laws of Vermont *to 1834, wrote the first history of Montpelier at the request of the townspeople, wrote ten novels including the famous* Green Mountain Boys, *and prepared a number of articles for the periodical press.*
>
> *He cared little how he dressed, and was less careful in the way he chewed his tobacco. He would leave his Barre Street home and stroll downtown in his bedroom slippers, always walking exactly in the middle of the road. Despite his unusual habits, he was a highly respected member of the community and the village children loved him, for he always took time to stop and tell them a story of earlier days.*

The *Green Mountain Freeman*, an abolitionist newspaper edited by Thompson from 1849 to 1856, summed up the local attitude toward his *History of Montpelier* succinctly:

> *In his prime of life he was identified with almost every incident of our town history. Several years since, at the request of the town he prepared and published its history, which work is in many respects the most perfect of his writings. Interwoven with minute statement of fact, records and dates, are incidents of the earliest settlers, trivial in themselves, perhaps, but interesting to our citizens and calculated to endear our home to us all, and to perpetuate the memory of those most stalwart men of our earlier history. In a series of biographical sketches accompanying the history he has with great truthfulness and a keen appreciation, portrayed with anecdote and illustration, the characters of our leading departed citizens. The work is an excellent record of our town history.*

Suffering the consequences of a stroke, Thompson died at his Barre Street home in 1868. The house was consumed by fire a few short years after his

This bench marks the grave of Daniel Pierce Thompson at Green Mount Cemetery. *PH.*

demise, and with the flames, his carefully written notes on the early history of Vermont were lost forever. Montpelierites may be thankful that his great history of their town was already in print.

His grave at Green Mount Cemetery is marked by an inviting bench with peaceful views of the Winooski Valley and the Vermont State House. Old Daniel invites us to sit and visit.

The Montpelier Fire

The Great Fire of 1875 Determined the Appearance of the City

Two calamitous fires in 1875 made Montpelier what it is today. In early May, after the second blaze, one could stand on the Rialto Bridge on State Street and survey the smoldering ruins on Barre Street, the intervening structures having been reduced to rubble. The consequence of the conflagrations—to rebuild the commercial district with brick—is responsible for the coherent look of the capital city's downtown. But the tragedies that were answered by Montpelier's handsome Victorian façades were also remarkable for their tales of heroism and pathos.

The first fire was discovered in a tin shop on Main Street at about 12:45 a.m. in early March. The building was owned by Montpelier artist Thomas Waterman Wood, who was living in New York City and enjoying a successful career as a portrait painter. His tenant, J.D. Clogston, had a workshop on the second floor, and it was assumed that embers from the tinman's furnace started the blaze as the furnace had been in use as recently as 5:00 p.m. that afternoon. Although two fire engines were immediately summoned and hoses extended to the North Branch of the Winooski, they were unable to control the fire, which spread to two adjacent structures. A third company of firemen arrived, and the conflagration was extinguished in an hour's time. "Two buildings burned to the ground and one pretty much burned out," reported the *Vermont Watchman*. "The firemen and citizens, who had worked nobly, were returning home congratulating themselves that the enemy had been subdued, and feeling that they had earned repose for the remainder of the night."

However, at 2:30 a.m. Montpelier's fire chief, General Perley Pitkin; John Page; and "a few others were standing in the passageway behind Messrs. Carlos Bancroft & Sons on Main Street, when Mr. Page called the General's attention to a light through the window just under the eaves in Ira Town's building. While they were still discussing whether or not it was a reflection from the burning ruins, the flames burst from the roof just above the window, and the flames began anew." The wood-framed structure was quickly consumed, and the fire spread to a brick structure owned by T.J. Hubbard. A slight breeze exacerbated the inferno, and Hubbard's commercial block was soon reduced to a pile of rubble. Meanwhile, the fire spread west, and General Pitkin, surveying the tired fire brigades, sent for assistance from Barre and Northfield.

An hour and forty-five minutes later, Torrent 1 from the Granite City arrived, pulled by a four-horse team. The effect of the Barre fire company was immediately felt. The engine was stationed on the ice of the North Branch, and its two streams of water caused the flames to subside, and "the people's hearts began to take courage once more." But by 7:30 a.m., "the remains of the Rialto Block fell on the ice bed of the river with a loud crash." The post office building was the last to burn, and that was only

Torrent 1, fire company from Barre. *VHS.*

partially consumed. By 8:00 a.m., the fire was "practically out and when the Barre company was relieved by the Northfield men—a half hour later there was little else than ruins and shells of buildings to play upon."

The *Watchman* noted the usual assemblage of loafers and spectators:

> *The sidewalk committee was very large, and the stern resolution with which its members resisted appeals to man the pumps was truly remarkable. Evidently appreciating that if everybody worked there would be none to look after the women and children, they continued to gaze steadily at the flames and to criticize the firemen. To judge from their remarks, better theoretical flame-quellers than themselves never existed; but they did not deign to give their fellow-citizens a practical test of their valor and skill. If ever a fire was stared out of countenance this fire was.*

On a positive note, the paper observed that, as the contents of buildings were emptied into the streets, most goods were found to be in "a very fair condition. There was very little larceny, and, in fact, a more orderly crowd is seldom seen at a fire." Thanks were extended to "the generous ladies who provided the firemen with hot coffee and crackers." The crackers were the signature product of the Cross Baking Company, which had been in business in Montpelier since 1828.

The *Watchman* had high praise for General Perley Pitkin, a veteran of both the gold rush in California and the Civil War, during the final years of which he served as Vermont's quartermaster general. "General Pitkin," the newspaper noted, "remained on duty twenty-one hours and discharged the arduous duties of his position without flinching." Pitkin was employed in a managerial position at the Lane Manufacturing Company. A biographical compendium, *Men of Vermont*, summarized his character: "Every movement in town or village matters that contemplated a true and probable progress received his support. He was a man of fine physique and commanding appearance, and his presence filled the eye. His own eye, dark and clear, beamed with kindness and glowed with power. His personal influence, born of the general respect which was had for his judgment and his fairness was very great—in a word it was a commanding influence."

The losses were detailed by the *Watchman*. On Main Street, four commercial structures were lost and six on State Street. "In all twenty business men and firms were burned out; three lawyers and one dentist were burned and four societies."

General Perley P. Pitkin, fire chief. *VHS.*

It is amazing to read of the resilience of the businesses that lost their stores and offices. Almost immediately, the affected firms had made arrangements for new quarters. "The first one to re-establish himself was Woolson, the tailor. He moved out the bulk of his goods before the fire fairly reached him, transferred them to rooms in Langdon's new block, over the First National Bank, and by nine o'clock on Friday morning [the day after the fire] had his sign out and was ready for business."

The second great fire, on the first of May, was far worse than the one in March.

It started at midnight where the March 5 fire ended—at Bruce's paint shop near Adams' Livery Stable on Main Street. The conditions were conducive to an accidental ignition, as there had been "no rain for several days, and everything was unusually dry; a strong south wind was blowing, which very soon changed to the west, and augmented by the fire itself, blew a perfect gale. The scene of the fire was a nest of old wooden rookeries, in the oldest portion of Montpelier, and it soon became evident that a sweeping conflagration was threatened."

As in the earlier blaze, General Pitkin, chief engineer of the fire department, was soon at hand and decided that it was not practical to save any of the wooden structures in proximity to the fire. He immediately sent to Barre, Northfield and Waterbury for aid. Pitkin identified the Frederick Marsh house and barn on the east side of Main Street as key to preventing the loss of the northeastern portion of the village. He charged Reverend Dr. Lord with command of the Engine No. 5 fire company with orders to stop the conflagration at this point. A bucket brigade was hastily formed to keep the barn wet while Lord and Captain Livingston, brandishing axes, entered the burning house. They fought their way to the loft and prevented the fire from spreading through the domicile.

> *At the same time, the south side of the house heated to crackling, and the men wrapped in wet carpets, played their hoses there as long as they could endure; then falling back for a rest, the attack was begun again. Three times did the furious flames threaten to gain the mastery, and as many times were they beaten back.*
>
> *So intense was the heat on the Preston building side, that without the use of wet carpeting, no man could possibly have lived even a minute, and even with that protection, it was discovered the next day that feet and legs had been badly blistered.*

The fight here lasted for over two hours. The *Caledonian* observed that Dr. Lord had begun the campaign as a respectably dressed clergyman, "wearing a nice tall hat and a shirt with a spotless bosom. He came out one of the most dilapidated men in town—hat drenched and squashed, face sooty, and clothes bedraggled. But the flames had been conquered, and the northeastern section of town had been saved."

Dr. William Hayes Lord was fifty-one years old and the highly regarded pastor of Bethany Church, as well as the president of the Vermont Historical Society. He had arrived in Montpelier shortly after his graduation from Andover Theological Seminary and, after preaching his first sermon on New Year's Day in 1847, was invited to lead the Congregational Church. He had received through the years many offers to serve larger churches throughout New England but elected to stay in Montpelier because (according to a Vermont Historical Society biography) "he loved the place where his children were born; he loved his

Reverend William H. Lord. *VHS.*

church and congregation with a strong and tender love; he loved the freedom and fellowship that prevailed in Vermont communities; he loved the green hills, the running brooks and pure air of his adopted state, and delighted when worn with study, fishing reel in hand, to follow the mountain streams in pursuit of trout."

Lord had graduated from Dartmouth before attending Andover—his father was the notorious president of Dartmouth, Nathan Lord, who gained infamy by supporting the South during the Civil War. William's tenure in Montpelier was without blemish, and he was to serve his congregation for two more years after the fire. He died in March 1877.

General Pitkin made his second stand against the fire at the Wells River Railroad Depot at the junction of Main and Barre Streets. He feared the loss of the depot would also mean the loss of the gristmill, the carriage shop and, ultimately, the railroad bridge over the Winooski River. "Two hundred thousand dollars worth of property depended on the fire's stoppage at this point." Humphrey Campbell, Frank Jangraw, Samuel Luck and Fred Butterfly played the hoses in turn on the burning buildings, the depot and then one another for four hours until the arrival of the Barre and Northfield fire brigades gave them an opportunity to rest.

Hyde's Block, the building at the corner of Barre and Main Streets, was discovered aflame, and the fire then "raged in two directions—up Barre and down Main streets, on both sides of each street." General Pitkin placed Colonel Randall in command at Barre Street, and having no engine to give him, his orders were to wage a hand-to-hand fight as best he could.

Colonel Francis Voltaire Randall was a distinguished veteran of the Civil War, having helped raise the Thirteenth Vermont Regiment and served as its colonel. He was cited

Reverend James E. Wright. *VHS.*

for meritorious service at Gettysburg, where the Thirteenth Regiment was instrumental in repelling Pickett's Charge. After the war, he returned to Montpelier to continue his career as a successful trial lawyer.

The battle on Barre Street soon divided into two—one at Joseph Silloway's, where Reverend J. Edward Wright was the leader, and the other at the Charles Lyman house, a substantial brick dwelling on the north side of the street.

"Pulling off his boots and stockings Mr. Wright mounted a ladder barefoot, and ascended to the ridgepole where he was held in place by a pair of reins thrown around a chimney." Two boys and a man mounted the ladder, and two lines of men with buckets supplied a steady supply of water. The carpeting around Mr. Wright's neck and the occasional bucket of water dashed over him allowed the minister to hold his ground and save the Silloway house.

A successful defense of the Lyman house across the street was led by Colonel Randall.

The colonel reported in the *Caledonian*

> *that while, as usual on such occasions, there was a mass of loafers who were wholly impervious to all appeals to fall in and help, either from paralysis or laziness, yet there was a body of resolute and energetic men, some seventy in number, and to them all praise is due. Mr. Wright proved himself a true hero, and in Col. Randall's opinion, no braver act was ever done, than his maintenance of the ridgepole of Silloway's house for two hours, in the midst of a shower of firebrands, and with the air so hot that it was only by wet carpets around his neck and head, and repeated dowsings with water, that he could survive.*

Reverend J. Edward Wright was born in Montpelier in 1839 and graduated from Montpelier Academy and Harvard. He prepared for the ministry at Andover but left to join the Forty-fourth Massachusetts Regiment. He was ordained in Illinois after the Civil War and became pastor of Montpelier's Church of the Messiah in 1869. He retired as pastor emeritus in 1911.

Reverend N. Newton Glazier also distinguished himself with Colonel Randall, who observed that "his one arm was worth more than the two that many men possess—men like the one the Colonel asked to fall into the line of bucket men and who replied that 'his clothes were too good.' The Colonel's acquaintances can imagine the adjuration that young man got."

Nelson Newton Glazier was from Stratton, Vermont, and educated at Brown University and Newton Seminary. He was a commissioned officer in Company A of the Eleventh Regiment of Vermont Volunteers and lost his left arm at Spotsylvania, Virginia, in May 1864. During the year of the Great Fire, he served as superintendent of common schools in Montpelier and was ordained as a minister in the Baptist Church.

It should come as no surprise that General Pitkin would seek out former military officers to execute his strategy for fighting the cataclysmic fire. What seems unusual, however, is that the majority of these veterans were clergy. It is likely that the pastors were more actively concerned with their community than other veterans who resided in Montpelier and their congregations looked to them for guidance and leadership.

In all, the fire lasted for three hours and burned about two acres of the town. In that brief time, the flames consumed, according to the *Watchman*, "forty buildings including blocks of stores, dwelling houses, barns, and sheds." Thirty-five families were left homeless. However, noted the *Argus and Patriot*, "Friends were found in abundance and before night all had been sheltered, as well as their most pressing needs attended to." Many merchants had moved their goods to the streets in advance of the flames. "Some removed a little out of their stores only to have it fall into the hands of robbers and plunderers, quite as heartless and cruel as the fire itself."

The *Argus* later observed:

> *This second fire, coming as it did, just as our citizens were bending renewed energies to remove the vestiges of the first, has cast an unwonted gloom over the community and the spring of 1875 must always be remembered as a black one for Montpelier—in which families were rendered homeless, merchants deprived of stores and goods, workmen thrown out of employment, the rich crippled, and the poor made to lose their all.*

The *Montpelier Argus and Patriot* lamented the loss of the city's historic buildings. "The previous great fire [in March] had swept away many of the old landmarks of the town" such as the well-known Shepard Tavern on South Main Street. It had been built by William Hutchins and was only the second tavern erected in Montpelier. In 1794, Williams's father opened a store on the site of the Tavern's stables. The Tavern had been a favorite stopping place for travelers from Boston heading to Montreal until the railroad rendered it unnecessary. "On the east side of the street the old time residences were far more numerous. The residence occupied by Mrs. Marsh was built before 1815 by Jacob Kimball. The Wood house next south was built some 10 years later by John Wood, father of Thomas Waterman Wood, the celebrated Vermont artist, and therein Mr. Wood lived until his decease." The account describes in detail the builders and the houses from the first decades of the city's existence and then lost forever, not the least of which was the Barre Street home of Colonel Miller, the "American Daredevil" who famously fought for Greek independence abroad and the abolition of slavery at home.

A city less susceptible to fire was a major concern for those wishing to rebuild Montpelier, and some of the capital city's first building codes were considered. Flat roofs were deemed more practical for firefighting than pitched ones, and noncombustible building materials were deemed preferable, as was regulating the construction and placement of chimneys. A long-awaited proposal for a municipal waterworks system was endorsed, as well as updating the city's antiquated fire engines.

The reporters for the *Watchman* and *Argus and Patriot* believed the May fire was deliberately set. No one was ever prosecuted for the arson.

The Lane Shops

Important Manufacturer of the Nineteenth Century

In Montpelier, we simply called it "the Lane Shops." From its heyday as a major Vermont manufacturer, the Lane Manufacturing Company's production capabilities had dwindled to almost nothing after World War II. Generations of schoolchildren, along with the occasional automobile crossing the bridge over the North Branch, had wandered through its complex of buildings from "the Meadow" to Main Street School and occasionally found a factory door left open on rusty hinges. A hurried glance inside revealed the diminished glory of an idle factory with cast-iron machinery, wide leather belts and cogs and gears begrimed with decades of dust and grease. It had, at one time, been the largest commercial enterprise in Montpelier, a city that boasted insurance titans and a nationally known print shop.

Dennis Lane, a sawmill operator from Barre, had settled his business in Plainfield, and by the 1850s, he had begun improvements to his machinery that would eventually revolutionize the world's sawmills. As tinkering with his equipment required ever more space, in 1863, he brought his enterprise to Montpelier to a location on Elm Street known as Waterman Falls—an early location for some of the town's first mills. One day, he happened to show his inventions to General Perley Pitkin, at that time chief quartermaster for the Army of the Potomac. Pitkin said nothing, but when he returned to the army, he told a friend that "he thought he had discovered the business that he should engage in 'when this cruel war is over.'" At the cease of hostilities, Pitkin joined forces with Lane. Dorman Kent, longtime chronicler of Montpelier, remarked of this partnership, "Lane provided the genius and

Dennis Lane (from *Gazetteer of Washington County*, 1889). *PH.*

The Lane Manufacturing Company, circa 1900. *PH.*

Pitkin supplied the capital." James Brock, offering legal expertise, would join them in a firm that became known as Lane, Pitkin and Brock. This consortium soon bought the land on which Lane's workshop stood, thereby securing the important water rights that it controlled. By 1872, the company had incorporated as the Lane Manufacturing Company with headquarters on Mechanic Street in Montpelier, an address it would claim for nearly one hundred years.

Lane had already patented his improved "Lever Set Circular Saw Mill," which quickly became the standard for sawmills nationally. His improvement facilitated cuts of a consistent thickness and a mechanical means for propelling a log through the innovative circular blade. A new "balloon framing" technique for building houses necessitated lumber of consistent and accurate dimensions, and Lane's Lever Set Circular Saw Mill fulfilled the necessary requirements. At that time, wrote the *St. Albans Messenger*, "they are making a large double mill, that is, a mill having two circular saws for Natchez, Mississippi; it will carry one 72 and one 40 inch saw and cut cypress logs 5 to 6 feet in diameter. One of the single mills can boast cutting over 4,000 feet of spruce boards in an hour." The improved mill was essential for feeding the great appetite of America's new industrial age.

The great innovator of the firm was Dennis Lane. Born in Barre in 1818, he found himself in Plainfield some forty years later operating a sawmill. He and his brother owned over two thousand acres of forestland, and both operated sawmills in an area along the Wells River Railroad line in Marshfield that became known as Lanesboro, named for the ambitious sawyers. It was said that he was a natural-born mechanic and, as a boy, whiled away hours fashioning waterwheels with a jackknife. A biographical sketch in the *Gazetteer of Washington County* (1889) paints an attractive portrait:

> *But he was not simply an inventor. He also had an acknowledged capacity for general business affairs, and had a mind of his own, which guided him in forming conclusions that were evidences of his good judgment. Mr. Lane was a silent, unassuming man, but a close thinker. He was independent in action, but very liberal in his treatment of those who differed with him in sentiment, either political or religious. He disliked ostentation, show, cant, and hypocrisy. His interest in the poor and pity for the unfortunate was proverbial. He not only said "be ye warmed, clothed, and fed," but in a substantial manner proved his sincerity, and was the author of many deeds of charity positively known only to himself.*

Left: Orleska Lane. *PH.*

Below: Residences at the Lane Shops. *PH.*

Lane married Orleska Freeman in 1844 and soon became also known as a "kind, considerate, generous, and indulgent" husband and father. He had started manufacturing his patented design sawmills on his own in a small way, but when he joined forces with General Pitkin, they found a hungry demand for their portable mills as the nation's soldiers put down their arms in favor of industry. Brock, also a returning Civil War veteran, supplied additional capital and legal expertise. Soon, a profitable and innovative corporation was launched that would eventually inhabit over seven acres with eleven buildings. By the time of Dennis Lane's death in 1888, Lane Manufacturing's payroll numbered over 150 employees.

The extensive complex of the Lane Manufacturing Company included a foundry, a forge and a machine shop. Later, a pattern house, an office and dwellings were added, including domiciles for workers. Today, most of the original structures remaining at the Mechanic Street location have been converted to condominiums and apartments.

As might be expected from a boy who fashioned waterwheels with a jackknife, Lane's mechanical expertise expanded to include water turbines, specifically "the Monitor" model, as well as planers and clapboard and shingle mills. The Lane Manufacturing Company supplied traveling cranes, polishers and saws to the stone sheds of the burgeoning granite industry in both Barre and Montpelier.

In 1888, Dennis Lane died just as the company achieved its apex of corporate growth. His loss was mourned by all of Montpelier's citizenry. The funeral was held at his family home on the corner of Elm and Vine Streets near his factory. The *Argus and Patriot* noted that the parlor was elegantly appointed for the occasion, and

> *the casket was as fine as money could buy, made of red cedar covered with black broad-cloth, heavily corded, and mounted with gold and silver ornaments, in which Masonic emblems were conspicuous. The interior of the casket was lined with the richest of cream-colored satin, and the body was dressed in a black suit. After the ceremonies at the house, Aurora Lodge of which some 50 members were present, took charge of the body, and the services of the tomb were according to the Masonic ritual.*

Interment was at Green Mount Cemetery.

Upon Lane's demise, General Pitkin and his three sons took over the daily operation of the company. Despite diversification into water turbines, woodworking and granite-working machinery, the Circular Saw Mill was its bread and butter. The mills were shipped to destinations as remote as a site in Peru, four thousand miles up the Amazon River.

The *Bennington Banner* wrote in 1891:

> *There is not in all New England a concern that approaches, in magnitude, the Lane Manufacturing Company. All of the principal buildings are brick, lighted throughout by electricity, and heated by steam, requiring about four miles of steam pipe. Power is furnished by water wheels, water motors and a 60 horse-power engine and boiler. The different departments of the works have been so admirably arranged with a view to convenience that there is no "false-motion" and no unnecessary delays or time lost in construction, setting-up, or shipping. The manufacture of the iron work, commencing at one end, and the wood work at the other, gradually progress toward the center, where the saw mills and other machinery are completed ready for shipment.*
>
> *The town generously agreed to close that part of Franklin Street which ran by the shops, the land then reverting to the company, and the company laid a street back of Franklin Street for the accommodation of the public. This enabled them to put up their additional buildings with a view to appearance and convenience, instead of stringing them along the banks of the river.*
>
> *The Lane Circular Saw Mills are shipped to all parts of the civilized world. In the past year mills have been shipped to South America, Cuba, British America, Uruguay, Paraguay, Chile, England, Sweden, Alaska, the great North-west, and the Pacific coast.*

Betsy Bouton's *History of the Lane Manufacturing Company* (1978) noted that the largest models "helped clear the Michigan woods and the small portable ones were moved around the Vermont forests." Many are still in use to this day. Bouton wrote that mismanagement by General Pitkin's three sons after his death in 1907 left the company vulnerable to the economic hardships of the Great Depression. Contracts for turning machine parts during World War II brought a fleeting renaissance, but orders diminished after the war, forcing the company to close in 1961.

For a time in the early 1970s, the second floor of the pattern house was opened as a nightclub called Blacky Stone's Industrial Revolution. A broadside advertising the bar purports that the name was derived from the tragedy of Blacky Stone, a night watchman at the Lane Shops, who hanged himself there in the early 1900s.

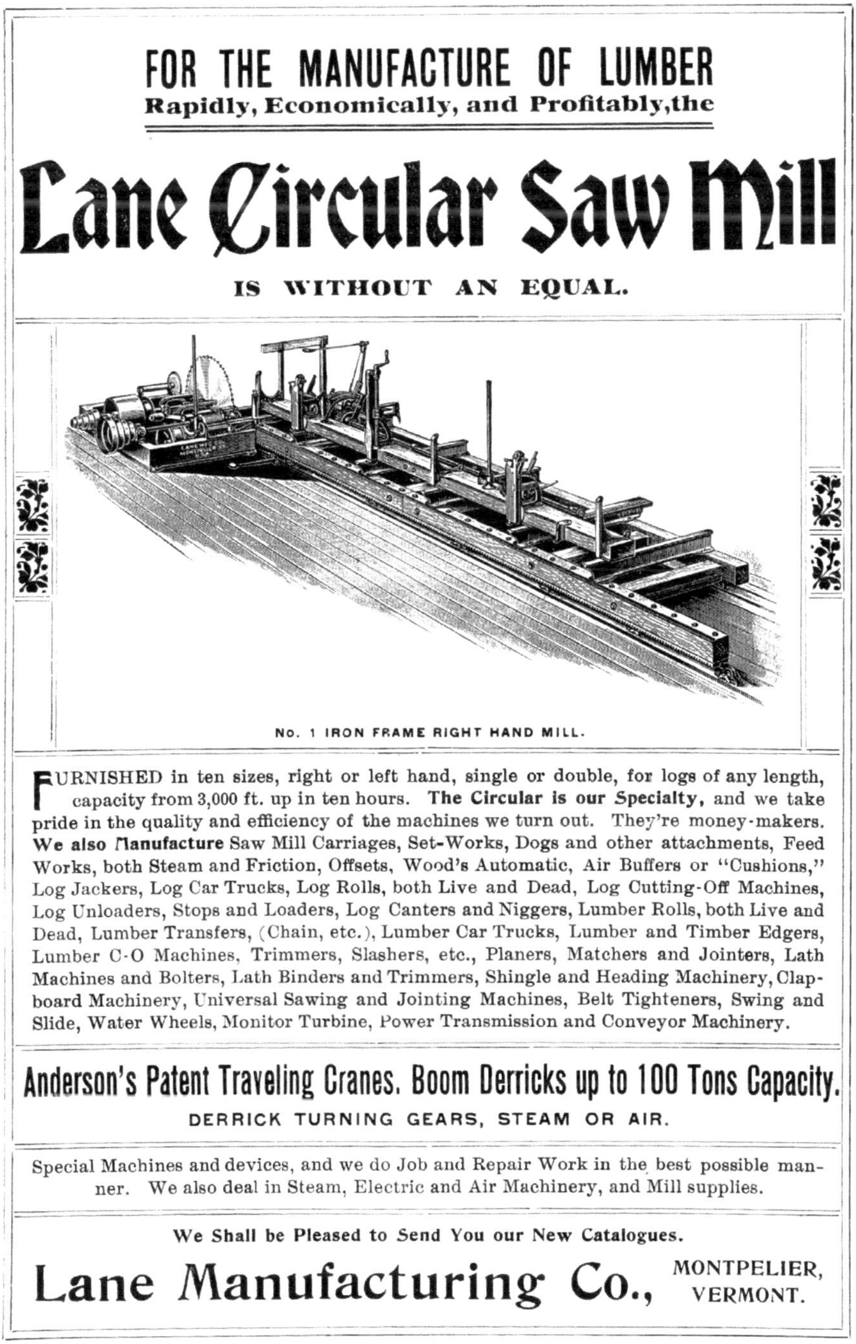

Lane Circular Saw Mill advertisement, 1905. *PH.*

In 1971, Denny Lane, great-grandson of the founder, bought part of the original property to manufacture replacement parts for Lane machinery. He continued in this enterprise until early 1977, when a fire destroyed his holdings at the Lane Shops.

The *Vermont Watchman Souvenir Edition* (1893) enthused, "To Montpelier this splendid industry has been a source of activity and wealth. Its workmen are representative of the most skillful, intelligent and thrifty order of American artisans, and have not only enriched the town by their labors but benefited it in many other ways through a patriotic and serviceable citizenship."

That which is left of the once bustling industrial hub of Montpelier recalls the clamor of hammer and iron that once rang through a great Vermont factory. Thousands of Lane sawmills are still in use, and the mechanized roar of their circular blades echo the tumult of manufacturing once heard on upper Elm Street in Vermont's capital city.

Joel Foster and the Waterworks

The New Water System Introduced after the Great Fire

When Joel Foster died in 1903, the citizens of Montpelier memorialized him in a way that no other resident of Montpelier has been honored. They adorned his grave in Green Mount Cemetery with an impressive monument paid for by public funds. The contract for the granite sculpture was awarded to T.J. Kelleher, whose winning bid was $998 for a sixteen-foot-high statue on a pedestal. Kelleher sublet the contract to Montpelier's great sculptor Harry J. Bertoli, and several plaster models were cast until one met with the approval of a citizens' committee. The completed monument is a full statue of Foster. In one hand, the figure clutches a derby hat while the other rests on a fire hydrant, a fitting pose for the father of Montpelier's water system.

Before 1885, a hodgepodge of wells, springs and privately owned water systems (such as John Hubbard's in the Meadow) supplied water to residents of Montpelier. Dorman Kent, Montpelier's indefatigable chronicler of events, recalled the day in 1884 when the water began flowing from Berlin Pond. "Great was the rejoicing and the outhouses and wooden tubs were soon broken up for firewood."

As the capital city grew, a central water system had been discussed as early as the 1850s. There was even a survey prepared in 1860 to explore the viability of an aqueduct from Berlin Pond to Montpelier. An initiative in 1872, led by the visionary Samuel Wells, presented a report that did not immediately receive favorable action. It detailed the desirability of a municipal water supply, but voters were reluctant to take on the tax burden.

Fire hydrant detail of Joel Foster statue. *PH.*

When calamitous fires in 1875 reduced the business district of the city to ashes, there was renewed interest in the project, and in 1883, the voters approved the sale of $50,000 worth of bonds to commence work on this great public works endeavor. In comparison, it may be noted that Burlington had supported a city water system since 1868.

A waterworks board was appointed, and it recommended taking the water from Berlin Pond in Berlin near the head of Benjamin Falls. The ongoing costs of the project were to be paid from rents charged to customers, and the system continued to expand until, by 1893, ten years after the project was initiated, almost eighteen miles of pipe had been installed.

As the construction commenced, the city hired Joel Foster to supervise building the waterworks. A self-taught engineer, Foster had been a hardworking selectman for Montpelier, an early officer of the Wells River Railroad, Montpelier street commissioner and, for fifteen years, chief of the Montpelier Fire Department. In 1893, it was noted in the *Montpelier Souvenir*, "His business ability, his good judgment and varied experience, his engineering skill, his capacity for much hard work and difficult service, have all found full scope in the management of this important public work. He takes a fatherly pride and interest in this later exhibition of the public spirit of the village, and to his watchful care and competent management a large share of the magnificent success of the Montpelier Water Works is justly attributable."

Joel Foster was born in Fayston, a small village near Waterbury, in 1825. Sporadically attending a district school, he was later highly regarded for his "strong common sense, native intelligence and self reliance." His innate abilities allowed him to serve as a schoolmaster for a few years, but by 1849, he had come to Montpelier to clerk in a hardware store owned by Edward D. Hyde. The enterprise at the corner of Main and Barre Streets consisted of two floors in a large building measuring twenty-five by seventy feet with a large basement and storage facility. In a few years' time, the young clerk had proven his value to Mr. Hyde, and the business became known as Hyde and Foster. Foster so admired Edward Hyde that he named his second son George Hyde Foster.

Joel Foster married Mary Ware of Montpelier in 1855. She was described by the *Argus* as "a woman of unusual ability and force of character." Their sons, Joel Ware Foster and G. Hyde Foster, grew to maturity in Montpelier and later migrated west to Cheyenne, Wyoming, and Omaha, Nebraska, respectively.

Foster left the firm in 1877 to devote his energies to his surveying business. The *Souvenir* observed, "He had surveyed and explored many thousands of acres of timberlands in Washington and adjoining Counties. Every mountain summit, every hillside and wooded range in central Vermont, has been traversed by him, and he will point out to the interested observer the exact locality of town lines, he will trace the course of every winding stream, locate every hill or mountain peak in view, call it by its name and give its height."

Henry Estabrook, renowned jurist and orator of Omaha, Nebraska, had the good fortune to meet Joel Foster when he visited Montpelier in 1894. Of Foster, he noted that he was "a man with the woodcraft of an Indian and the knowledge of a scientist. Every woodchuck hole he has located and explored; every birdsong he knows and what it portends of storm or sunshine; the altitude of every hill, the history of every building, every tree and shrub, and weed—all are as familiar to him as the faces of old friends."

In 1883, the news of the impending public works project had received regional notice. The *Boston Journal* thought it worthwhile to report on the project in Montpelier: "The most important work of the year will be the construction of the water works." The *Journal* described the effort to bring water through a twelve-inch main from Berlin Pond, some 325 feet in elevation above Montpelier. "Mains eight and ten inches in size are to be connected with the twelve inch pipe and these carried through all the streets of the village, including about eight miles of pipe in all. The water is of the best quality." The newspaper pointed out that since 1874 there had been over twenty fires in the city with considerable uninsured losses. Certainly, this was an important consideration in eliciting public support for the project. But the devastating fire of 1875 compelled the voters to give the proposal their endorsement.

The dam that created Montpelier's water supply at Berlin Pond. *PH.*

In a report to the city officers, Joel Foster discussed the parameters of the project. "Berlin Pond, from which we receive our water supply, contains an area of 231 acres. It is 970 feet above sea level, and has a water shed of about 6,000 acres. The Pond is supplied almost exclusively from the numerous springs surrounding it on every side, and has a storage capacity of thirty-two inches above the 'pine log' outlet, which can be drawn from as necessity demands, in a drought or otherwise." After determining that the proper place to take the water for the city was at the head of the falls, a number of manufacturing facilities had to be purchased because the city's demands would interfere with the hydropower required to run their machinery. By 1899, the city had paid damages to a chair factory, a hoe factory and a mill owned by a Mr. Bosworth.

Considering the scope of the project, the work proceeded apace despite the sort of problems that plagued large public works initiatives. A suit brought by S.W. Benjamin, who claimed the water power he harnessed at Benjamin Falls was compromised by the water supply intake, was settled for $700, an amount Benjamin found equitable. There were also problems with the labor force imported to dig the ditches for the water main. The sizable influx of transient workers had predictable results. On the weekend before the water from Berlin Pond made its first appearance in downtown Montpelier, the *Argus* reported a disturbance on lower Main Street:

> *Another disgraceful fight is added to the list of wrong doing in and about the Capital. Last Friday night a lot of the men who have been at work on the ditches of the Montpelier water works were the combatants. The insurrection began on South Main Street about 10:00 P.M., and, notwithstanding the vigilance of the Capital police, was continued to the Arch Bridge, where a regular knock down was engaged in. The party fought through the bridge, keeping up the disgraceful and brutal performance until after midnight, at which hour some ten or twelve were pounding, biting and kicking each other near the tannery.*

Once the water supply was properly functioning, the receipts from "water rents" amounted to over $15,000 yearly. Joel Foster, who served as superintendent for many years, was paid almost $4,700 in 1902—a sum amounting to well over $100,000 today.

While great thought was given to its water supply, Montpelier (like many valley towns) made little provision for wastewater; rather, it installed drainpipes that emptied into the North Branch and Winooski Rivers. During

Statue in honor of Joel Foster in Green Mount Cemetery (sculptor: Harry Bertoli). *PH.*

the dry summer of 1854, the *Montpelier Argus* observed, "the low condition of water in the Worcester Branch and the Winooski is terrible. Several sewer outlets are a number of feet from the water and deposit the sewerage in such a manner it is left on the ground to decompose in the sun. The stench is awful." Dorman Kent noted how little things had changed during the drought of 1893.

In 1912, Mayor Ballard said, "It would be a wise procedure to examine into the up-to-date methods of disposing of city sewage, bearing in mind that we cannot expect to use the public waters of the Winooski River as a means of carrying away the city's waste." The situation remained unimproved into the early 1960s, when young children were warned to stay clear of the riverbanks for fear of contracting water-born diseases. Certainly, no fish caught in the river were consumed. The situation remained unchanged until 1963, when a sewage treatment plant became operational.

The peace of Superintendent Foster's final years was interrupted by the mysterious disappearance of his son. Joel Ware Foster, reported missing in early 1898, was found wandering aimlessly on the streets of Chicago by a friend who had been sent from Cheyenne to find him. He was returned to Wyoming but later placed under the care of a physician in Chicago. Joel Ware Foster had been a representative of the National Life Insurance

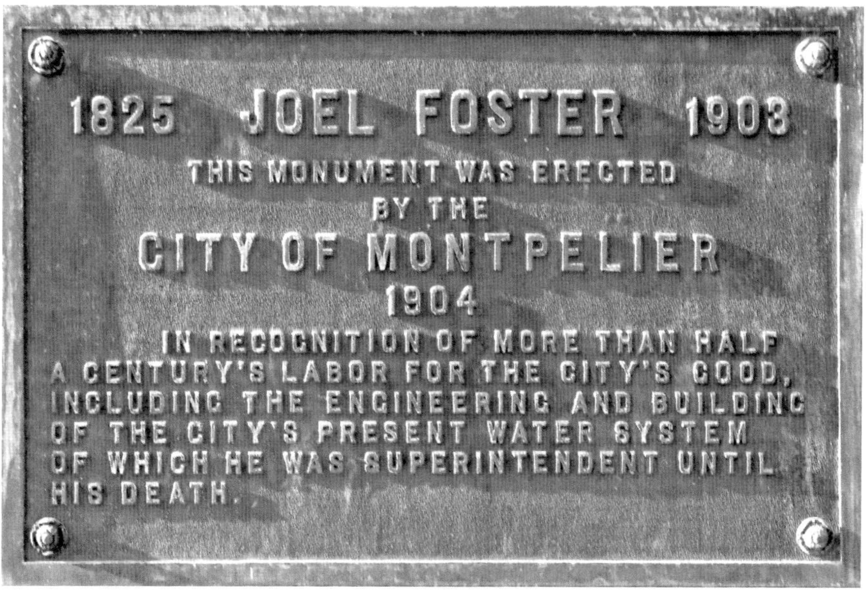

The bronze tablet on the Joel Foster monument. *PH.*

Company, as well as a bank officer. There were charges of embezzlement leveled against him, but he faced no criminal proceedings.

Joel Foster suffered from asthma, and he succumbed to complications from the disease on February 24, 1903. Soon after his death, the city select board commissioned the monument that marks his grave in Green Mount Cemetery. Widow Mary Foster lent her support to the project, and a plaster model by sculptor Harry J. Bertoli was featured in the city's 1903 Labor Day parade. It was met with resounding approval by the citizens of the capital city.

The statue stands atop a granite base with a derby hat clutched in the figure's left hand. This provides the only discordant note. As the monument was being installed, recalled Dorman Kent, some local citizens asked the contractor, "What was the idea of having Mr. Foster hold a derby hat in his hand, when he almost always wore a soft hat?" The contractor replied, "I didn't design the figure but how in hell could anybody make a soft hat out of granite?"

A bronze tablet on the monument reads "This monument was erected by the city of Montpelier in 1904 in recognition of more than a half century's labor for the city's good including the engineering and building of the city's present water system of which he was superintendent until his death."

Gould-Caswell Murder

The "Montpelier Murder" of 1889 Made National News

"Laura Cutler wants a divorce from the man she married after he had killed her husband on her wedding day." While the preceding might sound like the tortured plot of a soap opera, it was a national newspaper headline in late March 1891, summing up the essentials of what became known as the "Montpelier Murder," committed just over the town line in East Montpelier on the County Road. A reporter for the *New York Herald* wrote, "Those readers who do not believe in the theory of total depravity will have their disbelief badly tried by reading the story of this woman."

Laura Cutler was born in 1851 on her father's farm in East Montpelier—about one half mile past Cutler Cemetery. It was there that she first became acquainted with James Sherman Caswell, the hired man employed by her father, Willard Cutler. "Sherm," as he was popularly known, was a Civil War veteran who made the seventeen-year-old girl the object of his affections. In return, Laura was attracted to the handsome man. Wounded at Gettysburg, Caswell received a pension of twenty-four dollars a month, which supplemented his meager earnings as a farmhand. His romantic inclinations were, however, discouraged by Laura's father.

Dorman Kent, chronicler of daily life in Montpelier, recalled, "Sherm was in the habit of occasionally coming to town drinking and when so was inclined to be ugly." This may account for Willard Cutler's opinion regarding Caswell's suitability as a husband for his daughter.

Upon Willard's death, additional help was needed, and a neighbor, George Gould, was hired to help work the farm. Dorman Kent's father, Murray, was

Above: Laura Cutler and Sherm Caswell at the Cutler Farm. This photo was given to Dorman Kent by murderer Sherm Caswell. *VHS*.

Left: Murray Kent with his son Dorman. *VHS*.

executor of Willard's estate, and for various reasons, it took several months to settle. "In early September my father had practically closed it. By that time Miss Cutler had transferred her affections from Caswell to Gould." Seeing the warm relationship of Laura and the new farmhand, George Gould, Caswell pressed the woman for marriage, even giving her the funds to buy a wedding dress. Instead, she announced that she would be wed to George.

On the day of her marriage, Laura instructed Murray Kent to inform Caswell that his services on the farm were no longer needed and that he should also, after residing there for twenty-five years, find a new home. Kent told Caswell, "Now, Sherm, Laura has gone away to get married and you clear out before they get back. I have paid you in full all the estate owes you and clear out before they get back tomorrow." On Wednesday, September 4, 1889, Laura and George drove a horse and buggy the mile and a half to Montpelier, where they were joined in matrimony by the Reverend James Edward Wright, a Unitarian minister. They spent that evening with relatives in Putnamsville (now called Putnamville). Sherm Caswell, in a bitter, alcoholic rage, did not vacate the farm as directed but awaited their return on the following day.

On the morning of September 5, Laura and George Gould returned to the farm, and as Laura prepared some salt cod for lunch, Mr. Gould visited the woodshed to bring in kindling for the stove. As he mounted the stone step to the front door of the house, Caswell threw open a second-story window and lowered the barrel of a "heavily loaded shotgun to within about two feet of the head of the unsuspecting Gould, and fired. The victim gave a shriek as the charge of heavy shot ploughed through one side of his face, tearing it completely away, and penetrated his breast." Gould staggered to the far side of the road and fell, where he died a half hour later. So great was the blast that a piece of his upper lip, still bearing part of his mustache, was discovered near the doorstep. The *Montpelier Argus* reported, "The details of this crime are truly sickening, and caused even the strong men who arrived soon after its perpetration to turn pale and inwardly wish that they were anywhere else but at the scene of death."

When Laura heard the blast of the shotgun and her husband's cry, she rushed to the front hallway and, looking up the stairs, saw Caswell seemingly unconcerned. "Why—Sherm," she said. "What have you done?" Immediately, she realized that he had shot her husband. Fearing more violence, she fled the house for that of a relative and neighbor, Albert Cutler.

Caswell then descended the stairs, passing Mrs. Perry and Miss Winnie Cutler (the teenage daughter of Albert), who had stayed at the house while the newlyweds were away. Mrs. Perry said, in a frightened tone, "I'm sorry that you have shot George." To which he replied, "So am I."

He left the dwelling and proceeded to Horace Lawrence's house, where he asked Lawrence to hitch up his team and take him to the livery stable of Deputy Sheriff D.W. Dudley in Montpelier. Caswell said nothing of what had happened earlier at the Cutler homestead. Finding Dudley out of town on business, Caswell next sought police chief John Tuttle, but to no avail. He was finally arrested by Charles Deforrest Bancroft, who had learned of the shooting while shopping in a downtown store. He saw Caswell on Main Street, approached him and said, "Sherm, I hear bad reports about you." Caswell admitted that he had shot a man and had tried to turn himself in, first to Dudley and then to Tuttle, but could find neither one.

"I guess I shall have to take you into custody," said Bancroft. Assuring Caswell that he was a sworn officer, the man agreed to go with him. When Bancroft asked him who he shot, Caswell, at first, would not say. Bancroft asked if it was George Gould, and Caswell tearfully replied, "My God, I could not bear to think of that worthless fellow having her." He lamented the fact that he would in all likelihood hang for the crime and that he had no relatives to mourn for him. Then, speaking of the farm, he said, "All that is there is mine; it is my house and she is as much my wife as she ever can be of any other man; yet they told me to pack my things and get out, and I could not bear it."

They made their way to the county jail on lower Elm Street, and after locating the constable, Caswell was locked in a cell.

An autopsy was ordered at the first opportunity, and surprisingly, Dr. D.G. Kemp found that the head wound was not the cause of death; rather, the shotgun blast had traveled downward into the chest, and internal bleeding had filled the chest cavity with two quarts of blood. The reporter for the *Argus* noted that the weapon used was an old-fashioned shotgun, and "under the hammer was a fragment of the exploded percussion cap that was used the last time the gun was fired." Undertaker Turner then took the body to prepare it for burial. Placed immediately in a closed casket, it was noted that the widow of George Gould never saw the body of her slain husband after the shooting.

In an interview with the *Argus and Patriot*, the woman who, within the short span of eighteen hours, had been both a bride and a widow revealed that she had been on intimate terms with Caswell almost from the time he had begun living at the farm. She admitted that when "the time approached when it became apparent that Gould and Laura were contemplating an early marriage, Sherm began to grow savage. He drank heavily and abused her roundly." He maintained, while in his cups, that if she married George, he would kill him. Laura said that she believed this was an idle threat from one whose passions were inflamed with alcohol. The reporter noted that "the widow exhibited a remarkable degree of calmness throughout the entire proceedings and talked of the matters prior and subsequent to the proceedings with perfect composure, although she was very much broken down on the day of the murder."

The Saturday after the murder, the ceremonial services of Reverend James E. Wright were again requested, this time for the funeral of George Gould at whose nuptials he had recently presided. Burial was at Cutler Cemetery in East Montpelier.

Lurid reports from the trial in late March 1890 riveted the nation's attention as it was revealed that the "buxom" Laura had "lived with Caswell, her husband's murderer for 19 years occupying the relations of a wife, but never was married to him. She is very much in favor of Caswell, saying recently that she would marry him in a minute, if he was free. She has visited him frequently in jail, and held long conferences with his counsel." When a guilty verdict was delivered, she swooned in the courtroom, but recovered

The jail on Elm Street has been converted to offices for the Washington County sheriff's department. *PH.*

soon enough to marry her husband's murderer before the pronouncement of a sentence of life imprisonment.

She held Caswell's hand through the bars of his cell at Montpelier's county jail while a local justice of the peace, Hiram Huse, performed the ceremony. This was too much for the Wheeling, West Virginia *Register*, which announced the "Vermont Romance" as "A Blood Curdling Story from the Green Mountain State." Within months, the forty-year-old Laura realized that a marriage to a man serving a life sentence had certain limitations and filed papers for a divorce. There were also rumors that she was keeping company with a relative of her first husband, George Gould.

The newspapers reported that Laura received Caswell's pension for a while, but when she later sued for divorce, the payments were returned to Caswell's account. Over seventy years later, Winnie Cutler Wiggins, who was at the farm on the day of the murder, recalled, "Of course she married him for his pension money, which was quite a sum for those times." She added, "Gould was the more respectable of the two, but both had been much dissipated at times." Winnie dictated her recollections of the tragedy in 1959 while living in Orlando, Florida. She had learned that friends of hers spent summers in the Montpelier area and had met her great-niece, Florence Cutler. She thought that someone in the family should know the facts of the tragedy as she remembered them.

With his pension restored to him, Caswell announced plans to buy a monument for his grave and contracted with Charles A. Smith of Montpelier to supply one upon his death. In the fall of 1902, members of the local GAR (Grand Army of the Republic) chapter sought to secure a pardon for a fellow Civil War veteran who had been wounded at Gettysburg. The *Vermont Watchman* reported, "His old comrades in arms are endeavoring to make his last days comfortable." Another newspaper remarked, "The petitions submitted to the governor were signed by all the business men of prominence in Montpelier, Grand Army men, and members of the legislature from this county."

Caswell was pardoned in 1902 and lived his remaining years in Montpelier. His last address was at the Union House, a hotel on Main Street.

Laura remained on the farm, which was eventually sold to a lifelong bachelor, Lucius Gould (related to her first husband), for whom she kept house until her death in 1911. Her obituary noted that she had been born and had died in the same house in which the tragedy occurred. Both George Gould and Laura are buried at Cutler Cemetery, just down the hill from the Cutler farm. Laura rests on a hill overlooking the County Road. Down the row of headstones, less than ten feet away, lie the remains of her murdered husband, George.

In November 1902, in the days when teachers routinely boarded with families in town, a new teacher, Eunice Baker, arrived home after a day in the classroom. She had secured room and board at the Albert Cutler home just past Cutler Cemetery on the County Road. She had begun correcting students' themes when she was interrupted by a knock at the front door. "She went to the door and saw a tall, rather distinguished looking man standing there. He inquired if Albert was there." She invited him in and went to find Albert, who was very glad to greet the visitor. After pleasantries were exchanged, Caswell announced that he would walk to the cemetery to pay his respects at the grave of George Gould. When he left, Albert informed the teacher that the man who had just left was none other than Sherman Caswell, the murderer of George Gould. The young lady was terrified.

Caswell returned in short order and asked "for a pick axe and other tools and took them to straighten up George's gravestone." When Mrs. Cutler

Laura Cutler's grave *PH.*

George Gould's grave *PH.*

Sherm Caswell. *VHS.*

returned, Caswell was invited to supper and to stay the night as if it were the most natural thing to extend good-natured hospitality to a convicted murderer. Miss Baker's memories were recorded in a letter that eventually came into the possession of Florence Cutler, who continues to live in the area.

James Sherman Caswell died in Montpelier on March 21, 1917. He was seventy-four years old. Later that spring, he was buried in the Caswell family plot in Worcester, which was soon adorned with a fine granite monument.

Black Agnes

John Hubbard's Unquiet Grave

It is a Montpelier legend of disputable origin. The bronze statue memorializing the remains of John E. Hubbard in Green Mount Cemetery is said to be cursed. The fable has it that if one sits on the lap of the figure at midnight, misfortune will haunt anyone intrepid enough to so tempt fate. The statue by renowned sculptor Karl Bitter is, in local parlance, called "Black Agnes," due, among other things, to the dark verdigris tones of its weathered bronze. Popular accounts suggest that, in recent memory, three youths suffered the consequences of their reckless test of the curse. Peter Muise of Boston writes in his folklore blog, "One story claims that three teenagers sat on Black Agnes during the full moon, trying to show how brave they were. They all drove home safely that night and thought they had escaped the curse. But within a week one was in a serious car accident, one fell and broke his leg, and the third drowned when his canoe capsized in the Winooski River. Just coincidence or the malevolent power of Black Agnes?"

When John Hubbard, scion of one of Montpelier's first and most influential families, died in 1899, he was, very likely, the most hated man in town. His wealthy aunt Fanny Hubbard Kellogg had died a decade earlier, and she left the City of Montpelier her substantial fortune of over $350,000 (equivalent to $9 million today) to erect a chapel and gates at Green Mount Cemetery, as well as to build and endow a library to benefit the local citizenry. Fanny had no children, and John Hubbard, her closest relation, chose to contest the will to secure the inheritance for himself. In so doing, he earned the enmity of many of his neighbors and fellow citizens.

"Black Agnes." The sculpture by Karl Bitter adorns John Hubbard's grave at Green Mount Cemetery. *PH.*

Hubbard was by no means in need of money, having descended from Roger Hubbard, who had come to the settlement on the banks of the Winooski River in 1779. The Hubbard domain was in an area of Montpelier that was known as Hubbard's Meadow, and even after it became developed with homes, the prosperous neighborhood continued to be referred to as "the Meadow." Hubbard's obituary in the *Argus and Patriot* noted, "The line from which the deceased is descended were all shrewd business men." Hubbard's father, Erastus, had personally helped finance the building of the statehouse as well as the Pavilion Hotel.

Hubbard objected to the conditions of Fanny Kellogg's philanthropy on the grounds that "the will was irregular." The specific irregularity, he asserted, was that the witnesses did not know what they were signing. John Burgess, a summer resident of Montpelier (he had built Redstone as a seasonal cottage) was a close friend of Mrs. Kellogg and suggested in his autobiography that John Hubbard had bribed witnesses to support his side in the case. Furthermore, claimed Burgess, Hubbard bribed city councilors not to fight him in court and to accept a scaled-down version of a public library. Hubbard offered $30,000 to build a new library for Montpelier—less than one-tenth of what Fanny Kellogg had planned to leave to the city.

Burgess traveled to Montpelier in 1893 to support the intent of Fanny Kellogg's will and was dismayed at what he found. "I could easily detect the baleful influence stealing over the community. Men no longer looked each other squarely in the eye nor greeted each other with the hearty tones of innocence. I was distressed and confused in mind beyond measure."

John Hubbard prevailed in his legal challenge to Fanny Kellogg's will and began planning a new library for a fraction of the cost indicated in the Kellogg bequest. The combined efforts of Redstone resident John Burgess, local artist Thomas Waterman Wood and others frustrated Hubbard's attempts at establishing an "official" public library for Montpelier, and by the time of Hubbard's death, the status of his modest plans were unrealized.

To many residents of Montpelier, the demoralizing "baleful influence" continued until Hubbard's death at age fifty-three, when the extraordinary contents of his will were reported in the *Montpelier Argus and Patriot*. While the official cause of Hubbard's untimely death was given as liver cancer, there were those who believed it was the continued strain of his public dispute that led to his early passing.

To the surprise of many, his public-spirited bequest appeared to be an act of contrition for his greed-driven obstruction of Fanny Kellogg's wishes. In an article with the heading "Not Understood," the newspaper marveled

Hubbard Chapel at the entrance to Green Mount Cemetery. *PH.*

at his legacy. "With his death comes a revelation of what kind of a man he was, a revelation that fills many hearts with regret that their judgment was so harsh or that they had not better understood the man." His will stipulated $125,000 for a new library, $25,000 for a chapel and gates at Green Mount Cemetery, $85,000 to establish Hubbard Park, various distributions to nieces and $10,000 for a monument to mark the family cemetery plot. This was a substantial bequest, even from a citizen whom the *Argus* claimed was the "largest individual taxpayer in Montpelier." Pundits were too polite to mention that his will essentially fulfilled the original intent of his aunt Fanny Kellogg.

The executors of the Hubbard estate immediately began preparing for a monument to adorn his grave in Montpelier's most beautiful cemetery. Green Mount Cemetery was dedicated on September 15, 1855. Its creation was, undoubtedly, influenced by the "Rural Cemetery" movement of early to mid-nineteenth-century America. As burying grounds in most New England cities were nearing capacity, a movement toward more rural cemeteries, situated on the outskirts of town, was becoming fashionable. This, in turn, allowed for cemetery planning and design in ways that were heretofore unavailable in the limited confines of downtowns. In Montpelier, overcrowding at the Elm Street Cemetery was so severe that when Green Mount opened, many remains were disinterred and transferred to the bucolic location newly established on lower State Street. Denizens of the capital city

Clover Adams memorial in Rock Creek Cemetery, Washington, D.C. *Library of Congress.*

were justly proud of Green Mount. The 1893 *Montpelier Souvenir* extolled its assets: "The great glory of Montpelier is its cemetery, both for what it contains, its beauty of situation, and the perfection of its maintenance. Most of the chief actors in its history lie buried there."

Throughout the country, these rural cemeteries were seen as places for quiet reflection and for honoring and remembering the loved ones who had passed on. Eventually, they became destinations for significant memorial art or "funerary sculpture," as scholar Cynthia Mills expertly recounts in her 1996 doctoral dissertation. Mills delineates the circumstances of, perhaps, the most famous American cemetery sculpture of all time, the Adams Memorial in Washington, D.C.'s Rock Creek Cemetery.

Henry Adams, famous for his account of a life of privilege, *The Education of Henry Adams*, commissioned the great American sculptor Augustus Saint-Gaudens to create a tribute to his wife, who died by her own hand in 1885. The bronze memorial caused an immediate stir and became a popular tourist attraction in the nation's capital. Countless newspaper and magazine articles featured the sculpture, and photographs were sold by mail to individuals throughout the country. Cynthia Mills stated its importance:

> *The Adams monument became an important model for the type of unusual, major cemetery monument that men of achievement or of culture could aspire to commission, in effect buying "genius" and "taste" to separate them from the masses. In its use of bronze rather than stone, it associated itself with cosmopolitan European sculpture. In its move away from mid-nineteenth century euphemisms and the sentimentality associated with outdated style, and its embrace of the mysteries of the hereafter instead of the answers it became a touchstone for many future memorials.*

The executors of Hubbard's will were charged with providing a monument to adorn his grave in Green Mount Cemetery. William Paul Dillingham, governor of Vermont from 1888 to 1890, and Arthur D. Farwell served as co-executors, but it was Dillingham who shouldered much of the responsibility for the monument. A member of both the University of Vermont and National Life boards, Dillingham was worldly. He would certainly have known of the importance of the Adams Memorial and how art may both honor and redeem a life. Dillingham very likely used his contacts in academia to identify an artist for Hubbard's memorial.

He commissioned Karl Bitter to execute the artist's first cemetery statue. The Viennese sculptor had had a studio in New Jersey since 1889 and would have been impressed by the acclaim of Saint-Gaudens's sculpture for Henry Adams. The similarities of the two works are striking. Cynthia Mills notes the resemblance:

> *The bronze figure for the Hubbard memorial is a seated male figure, with head thrown back and eyes closed. He is covered with voluminous drapery, which as in the Adams memorial, suggests another realm but is not fixed in*

any time period. As in the Adams figure, one side of the figure's upper torso is exposed. The figure, just thirty inches deep and open in the back is set against a gray granite stele, which is lower and more horizontal than that in the Adams monument, with even less ornament.

The inscription on the exedra wall framing the figure from the back contains lines from William Cullen Bryant's famous poem "Thanatopsis" (Thoughts on Death), which would have been known to all literate Americans of the nineteenth century:

Thou go not like the
Quarry slave at night
Scourged to his dungeon
But sustained and soothed
By an unfaltering trust.

Approach thy grave
Like one who wraps
The Drapery of his couch
About him and lies down
To pleasant dream.

The lines suggest that Hubbard did not die in shame but met his death with a clear conscience.

Although the Adams figure was popularly called *Grief* and the Hubbard statue formally called *Thanatopsis*, there were, as Mills indicates, other important similarities between the two sculptures. The two pieces were so conflated in the minds of the average Montpelier resident that when Mrs. Sumner Kimball wanted to buy an even-tempered horse in 1902, recalled Dorman Kent, she thought a good test of its calmness would be a drive to Green Mountain Cemetery. "Drive me up to that new monument called 'Grief' at Johnnie Hubbard's grave," she told the seller. "And if she don't shy at that, I'll take her."

The notion that the sculpture was eerie or frightening persisted, and the legend of Black Agnes arose. Or did it? The shrouded figure over Hubbard's grave is clearly masculine, so how did it become "Agnes?" It seems that the Montpelier folktale has origins in another city five hundred miles to the south.

Statues inspired by the Saint-Gaudens sculpture and blatant imitations of it proliferated after the noteworthy appearance of the Adams memorial.

One unauthorized reproduction of the famous statue was prepared to mark the grave of a Civil War officer, Brevet General Felix Agnus of Baltimore. Homer Saint-Gaudens, the artist's son, wrote of the travesty: "A man named Felix Agnus of Baltimore, Maryland, the owner of the *Baltimore Star* [newspaper] immediately upon my father's death took advantage and ordered a gross and ill modeled copy of the work to be set up in his own lot in Druid Ridge Cemetery in Baltimore."

Agnus hoped the monument would distinguish his grave and, thus, his memory. But quite the opposite happened, as Mills points out:

> *Within a decade of Felix Agnus's death, urban legends that the statue was somehow haunted began to develop around the monument, which became known as "Black Aggie"* [or "Black Agnus"]. *Legends developed that "Aggie's" eyes would turn red and glow at midnight and that she let out a blood-curdling scream against the background sound of clanking chains. Tales were told of several instances in which people who had dared sit in the statue's lap after dark were later found dead. It thus became a teenage challenge to clamber into the statue's lap during late-night visits and to relate harrowing accounts of what happened.*

Although the tale of Montpelier's Black Agnes (or Agnus) is little more than a folktale ignominiously borrowed from another cursed grave, the true story of John Hubbard's greed and attempts at salvation through public works is just as haunting. And it bears the distinction of being true, as well.

The Keeley Institute

Treating Substance Abuse at the Turn of the Century

"A Baby Morphine Fiend," declared the headline in the *Montpelier Argus.* The June 1, 1893 newspaper reported that the case of addiction was unprecedented for Dr. J.W. Nichols of the Keeley Institute, a treatment center for alcoholics and drug addicts located at 110 State Street in the capital city. The rehabilitation facility had opened a year earlier in the rooms above the Vermont Mutual Fire Insurance Company, a handsome Georgian-style brick building across the street from the Pavilion Hotel. The *Argus* noted that Mrs. Nora Woodworth of Jonesville had appeared for treatment for her morphine addiction at the institute two weeks earlier. She was accompanied by her three-year-old daughter when the doctors discovered that the child was also suffering from the disease of opiate addiction. "Mrs. Woodworth is the mother of nine children and has been a victim of the morphine habit for four years," said the *Argus*. "When she was nursing the child she was taking 15 grains of morphine a day, and the little one, through its mother's milk became an innocent victim of the habit. When she was weaned, at the age of 10 months, it was necessary to give her morphine regularly, and when she came here for treatment, she was taking a grain and a half a day."

The twin scourges of alcoholism and drug abuse were rife in the nineteenth century. Morphine was one of the few effective medicines in doctors' pharmacopeia, used to treat everything from chronic pain to diarrhea. Opium was sold as an over-the-counter drug in general stores, and many patent medicines contained both alcohol and opiates and were available without the requirement of a prescription. Addiction treatment was often harsh and

The back of a brochure promoting Keeley Institute. *Sheldon Museum.*

dangerous. In the era before anticonvulsive medication, withdrawal from alcohol addiction could have lethal consequences. As a result, it was often the custom to use beer to wean alcoholics from their dependence on intoxicants.

The Keeley Institute was a franchised treatment center that used a novel approach to detoxification and sobriety. The "Keeley Cure," the brainchild of Dr. Leslie Keeley, relied on injections of "bichloride of gold" and a supportive and humane facility that characterized the state of addiction as a disease rather than a character flaw. Treatment at the various centers around the country was modeled on that of the flagship site in Dwight, Illinois. New arrivals were "introduced into an open, informal environment where they were first offered as much alcohol as they could imbibe." All patients received injections of bichloride of gold, a secret compound, four times a day in a course of treatment that lasted four weeks.

It has been reported that, as a child, novelist William Faulkner traveled to a Keeley center in Memphis, Tennessee, where his father was being treated for alcoholism. The Faulkner family enjoyed the sights of Memphis while father Murray was under the care of Keeley Institute physicians.

While many medical professionals sneered at the unorthodox practices advocated by Dr. Keeley, the institute was known to have provided successful outcomes to hundreds of victims of the dreaded malady. In the era before Alcoholics Anonymous and psychotherapy, it afforded solace to lost souls whose lives had been ravaged by addiction. It, notably, brought the malady out of the shadows of humiliation and shame, and its treatment of the condition as a disease heralded a new course for rehabilitation of alcohol and opiate addiction.

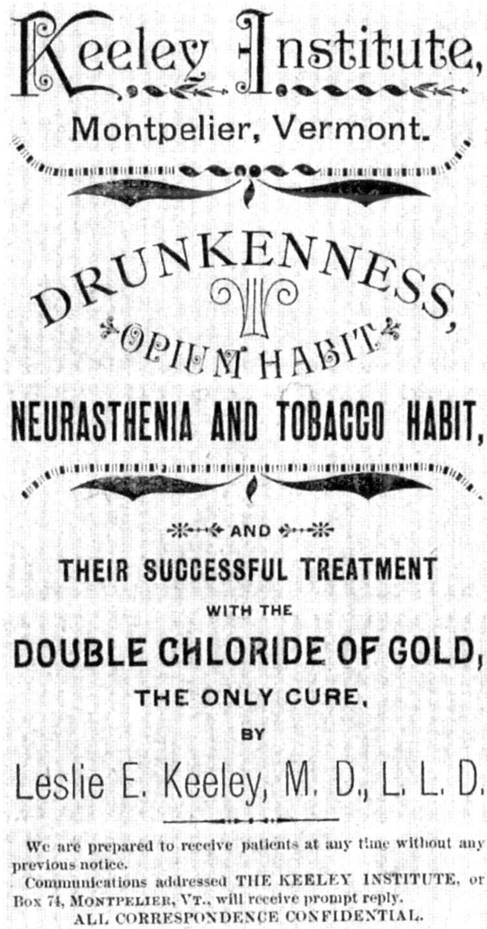

Cover of a brochure promoting the Keeley Institute in Montpelier. *Sheldon Museum.*

Montpelier's chronicler of contemporary life Dorman Kent noted that a cure at the institute had become, to an amusing degree, a measure of having *arrived* in polite society in the capital city. He observed in his newspaper column that, by 1893, "the Keeley Institute for the cure of the liquor habit was doing a rushing business in the Vermont Mutual Fire Insurance company building. Montpelier went so crazy over it. It became all but a distinction to take the Keeley cure."

Montpelier's franchise for the Keeley Cure opened to great acclaim in August 1892. Reporters from the *Montpelier Argus* interviewed the principals, business manager Charles Foster and physician J.W. Nichols.

> *The former is a gentleman of high character and fine business ability who devotes his personal attention to the management of the institute. He is himself a "graduate" and is enthusiastic in the work of aiding unfortunates to find relief from their afflictions. Dr. Nichols is a graduate of Bowdoin College and of the Maine Medical School. He has had a large and successful experience in the practice of general medicine and under the personal training of Dr. Leslie E. Keeley at the parent house in Dwight, Illinois, acquired a thorough knowledge of the methods of treatment there.*
>
> *Having purchased from the parent house at Dwight, the exclusive right of the state of Vermont to administer the Keeley Cure, Montpelier was selected as the location of the institute. Its central location, its excellent*

> *railroad communications, its fine hotel accommodations, its healthy climate, pure water, beautiful residences and public buildings, and its maple and elm shaded streets, all combine to make it one of the most charming locations in New England for a Keeley Institute.*

The second floor of the Vermont Mutual Fire Insurance building served as a social center for those undergoing treatment. The weekly numbers varied from twelve to forty as demand fluctuated. Upon arrival, patients were given a medical examination by Dr. Nichols and then administered regular doses of tonic and injections of the institute's secret gold preparations, "and, if he so desires he is furnished with the best whiskey so long as he cares to drink it. Some of the patients the first day or two drink a pint or more during 24 hours. At the end of the third or fourth day the liquor is voluntarily given up." The patients were not confined to the rooms of the institute but were free to walk around Montpelier and enjoy the amenities that the town had to offer.

Patients usually selected their own accommodations, most staying at nearby hotels such as the Pavilion, which offered privacy and discretion, as well as comfort. Some elected to rent a room in a private home. The institute recommended special accommodations for ladies: "There are several first-class boarding houses in town, in which lady patients can find pleasant accommodations and receive private treatment."

There were no restrictions on what patients did on their own time. Many enjoyed the natural beauty of central Vermont, enjoying the same activities as would any other visitors to the capital. "The knowledge that they are free from the clutches of drink comes to them like a benediction from heaven, and there is today no happier class of men in Montpelier." A promotional brochure extolled the citizenry of the capital:

> *Ever since the opening of the Keeley Institute in Montpelier, the citizens have manifested the greatest interest in its workings and welfare, and have heartily cooperated with the management at every opportunity, doing everything within their power to promote the best interests of the institution and its patients. The people of Montpelier rejoice over the good work going on in their midst. They bid the newcomer welcome, and words of encouragement and good cheer greet all.*

In contrast to the quiet anonymity of Alcoholics Anonymous (founded in Ohio in 1935 by two former Vermonters) many "graduates" of the Keeley Cure were outspoken advocates of the treatment. When asked by the *Argus* if their names could be used in their report, many prominent men around Vermont readily agreed to serve as enthusiastic proponents of the institute.

These "living advertisements" included G.W. Baker of Johnson, who was profiled in the *Argus*: "He was a victim of the morphine and liquor habit, and had been bedridden some time from their excessive use. He is [a] well-known citizen of the northern part of the state, and when he came to Montpelier was unable to walk without a cane, and his friends predicted that he would be taken back to Johnson in a box. He was a physical wreck while his friends today would hardly recognize him. He cannot say enough in favor of the treatment."

Newspapers throughout Vermont reported the visits of their citizens much as they announced vacations and business travel, and "graduates" of the program gathered for public reunions that helped reinforce their commitment to sobriety and served as an advertisement for the Keeley Cure. As Dorman Kent intimated, it seems that the Keeley Institute was a trendy destination for those who could afford treatment, room and board in the beautiful environs of Vermont's capital city.

A Women's Auxiliary Keeley League was formed, and regular meetings were held at members' homes. Apparently, it was a support group for the spouses of those afflicted serving much the same purpose as Al-Anon does today. Recalled Kent forty years later, the "Ladies Auxiliary Keeley League gave a lawn party in August of 1893, and the Montpelier Military band furnished music. The Ladies Auxiliary Keeley League was made up of wives of boozers who had taken the cure and many of our first families belonged. Then, when the old man quit drinking, the wives and daughters joined a league and made merry. Now some of the wives and some of the daughters make merry doing exactly what the old man tried to stop doing 40 years ago."

The Keeley Cure appeared to have won the endorsement of the local chapter of the Woman's Christian Temperance Union, inasmuch as they paid ninety dollars for the treatment of an indigent man from Barre. At a meeting in August 1893, they proffered their official endorsement, "pledging support in all possible ways."

The prominence of the Keeley Institute may be inferred from the "Grand Rally" held in November 1892. Led by the Montpelier Military Band, hundreds of graduates and well-wishers made their way up State Street from institute headquarters across from the Pavilion Hotel to the Blanchard Block Opera House, near the junction of Main and East State Streets. The *Argus* reported that one thousand people were in attendance with spectators standing in the aisles and at the back of the hall. Local attorney and

Alumni in recovery gather to march from institute headquarters to the Blanchard Opera House on Main Street. *VHS.*

Keeley alumnus William A. Lord presided over an evening of testimonials interrupted by cheers, applause and selections from the brass band.

Lord was just one of the many distinguished citizens of Montpelier who spoke that night. Born in 1849 and a graduate of Dartmouth, he was a prominent lawyer, state representative (Speaker of the House) and senator. He was the son of a prominent Montpelier clergyman and grandson of Nathan Lord, president of Dartmouth. He led the testimonials in a now-familiar confessional style, asserting that the Keeley Cure had saved his life. To thunderous applause, he introduced speaker after speaker who told similar stories. Among them was recovered morphine addict G.W. Baker of Johnson.

"I was using about fifteen grains of morphine and one and one half pints of whiskey per day when I came for treatment," he proclaimed. "And less than two weeks later, the chains with which I had been bound for years were broken."

Despite the popular acclaim the Keeley Cure engendered in Montpelier, there was disagreement about the institute's efficacy in the battle against addiction. Many physicians objected to the notion of the "magical elixir" in

Right: Prominent Montpelier citizen William Lord vouched for the Keeley Cure. *VHS.*

Below: The Keeley Institute today houses the State of Vermont Department of Human Resources. *PH.*

the form of bichloride of gold. Chemical analysis revealed that it contained a variety of compounds (with the exception of gold), and Keeley remained mute regarding his secret formula. An independent survey revealed that 51 percent of Keeley patients remained drug or alcohol free for the long term, a not-insignificant success rate but one far lower than Keeley's promotional matter claimed. Finally, competing recovery franchises assailed the Keeley Cure at every opportunity. Into this maelstrom were allegations that Charles Foster, business manager of the Montpelier franchise, had somehow embezzled funds and shortchanged patients. Dorman Kent caustically observed that the institute was "the finest managed graft ever seen in this place." The allegations were apparently unfounded, but the damage had been done, and Montpelier's Keeley Institute closed its doors in late January 1895.

In the few short years of its existence, more than five hundred patients had been treated for addiction. More importantly, the concept of addiction as disease would transform therapy for the coming century, paving the way for compassionate treatment for victims of substance dependency.

Clang, Clang, Clang Went the Trolley

A Brief History of the Electric Railroad Between Barre and Montpelier

George Murch passed around a box of Manila cigars to the crowd of invited dignitaries. The cigars had been a gift from Admiral George Dewey, "the Hero of Manila Bay," who had recently visited his hometown of Montpelier. This august assemblage had come together for the first trial run of the Barre and Montpelier Traction Company's streetcar service linking the two central Vermont municipalities. Murch was the superintendent of the Worcester Construction Company of Massachusetts, builders of the electric trolley line. To celebrate the maiden voyage of the streetcar, Murch had invited the mayors and aldermen of the two cities, as well as the selectmen of Berlin. Other guests swelled the party to over sixty, and the car was filled beyond its normal capacity. "With a score or more of youngsters clinging to all projections, the car made a successful trip from the car barn to Bolster's block at Barre and then to the Pavilion in Montpelier," reported a local newspaper.

The throng had gathered on June 27, 1898, at the car barn, the traction company's headquarters, located near the present roundabout on the Barre-Montpelier Road. It was a warm Monday afternoon, and before boarding the open streetcar, they toured the facility and listened to an explanation of the workings of the storage batteries that were called upon for extra power when the cars negotiated the steep tracks on Washington Street in Barre or Sibley Avenue in Montpelier. At a little past five o'clock that afternoon they boarded the car. Murch, serving as motorman, drove them to the Granite City, where "the streets were packed with people who kept up a continuous

A trolley at the "Y" in Barre. *VHS.*

cheering and waving of flags as the car passed along. Several horses made a decided objection to the innovation, but none of them got beyond the control of their drivers." When the car approached City Hall Park, it was reversed, and the trip to Montpelier was commenced. "From the foot of Barre Street to the Pavilion the streets of Montpelier had the appearance of a circus day. The walks were lined with people, all deeply interested in what will soon cease to be a novelty." The *Argus* also remarked that the city councilors of Barre and Montpelier, in a gesture of solidarity, joined hands on the trip and joked and jollied among themselves, appearing to have "a high old time." In closing, the *Argus* reporter predicted, "One of the pleasant features about the cars will be that they will promote more friendly and better relations between Barre and Montpelier and make the cities, as they should be, better acquainted with each other."

For a few decades in the early twentieth century, initially for five cents and later a dime, one could avail oneself of regular trolley service between Barre and Montpelier. The Barre and Montpelier Traction Company employed electric cars running on 9.2 miles of tracks placed in the middle of the main thoroughfares of the two cities. Although a popular means of transport with a ridership of almost one million passengers a year, the commuter line struggled financially and was never the financial windfall its owners had hoped for. Obstacles to its viability ranged from boycotts and labor disputes to weather-related calamities that finally rendered it impractical.

A trolley by the post office in Montpelier. *VHS.*

Electric railways or streetcar lines had been in existence only since the 1880s, and earlier versions employed horse or mechanical power. The first electric vehicles utilized a concept first articulated by Williamstown, Vermont native Thomas Davenport in 1834. Power was delivered to the electric motor through "trolleys" that attached the cars to overhead power lines. It took, however, the proliferation of electric power plants built for lighting and other domestic uses to make the streetcars a popular alternative to coal- and wood-powered locomotives and a logical means for moving people between neighboring cities. The *Montpelier Argus* noted in 1902, "The peculiar advantages of the electric system of traction are frequent service, flexibility, convenient location, clean, light and airy cars, and low fare. Of these probably the most important are location and the ability to maintain a frequent service with small units. By these means electric roads have succeeded where traffic did not previously exist and could not have been produced by steam roads."

The harnessing of hydropower from the Winooski River at a site just upstream from Montpelier's Pioneer Bridge enabled plans for a trolley line to be proposed. In 1886, the Standard Light and Power Manufacturing Company was organized "for the purpose of lighting the streets, public and private houses in Barre and also furnishing motive power and constructing and operating electrical railways." The power company soon sold the "motive power" rights to the newly organized Barre and Montpelier Traction Company. Part of the sales agreement was a stipulation, later proven to be consequential, that the Traction Company not purchase power from the Jesse Viles power plant in Middlesex, a competitor to the local power company.

An important investor in the Traction Company was entrepreneur J.J. Flynn, remembered today for the handsome theater on Burlington's Main Street that bears his name. Flynn was also involved in the organization of the Chittenden Trust Company and Green Mountain Power. Almost from the onset, Flynn and his cohorts were at odds with the perceived needs of the citizens of central Vermont and the ongoing tensions between the aldermen of Barre and Montpelier, and the traction company was to be a constant irritant to both.

These were boom years for trolley lines throughout America. Fortunes were made by owners of the lines who were savvy enough to include real estate development in their business models. These commuter rail lines facilitated the development of suburbs and tract homes, but the owners of the Barre and Montpelier Traction Company had other plans. They developed attractions between Barre and Montpelier to encourage riders and hoped to profit from paid attendance at their "amusement park." On June 1, 1898, almost one month before the trial run of the streetcar, Murch announced plans for Dewey Park, "extensive pleasure grounds to be fitted up beside the Winooski." Named for Montpelier's favorite son, Admiral Dewey, the bucolic retreat was adjacent to the traction company's car barn at what is today the intersection of Routes 2 and 302. "Swings, settees, and rustic seats will be placed in the woods, a bandstand will be erected, electric lights will be installed, frequent concerts will be given and various attractions will be devised for the enjoyment of the people who visit the place." Presumably, the visitors will have each paid a nickel for a ride to the destination on the streetcar. It was announced in August that Angelo Scampini, Barre's great entrepreneur, would soon move his merry-go-round there. The traction company also developed a baseball field about one hundred yards south of Dewey Park where teams from Montpelier and Barre would play for paying fans on Saturday afternoons.

The festive environs of Dewey Park and the Intercity Park Ball Field belied the hostilities that plagued the building of the line from the onset. These conflicts have been detailed in a manuscript by Tom Borrup held in the archives of the Vermont Historical Society. Barre officials felt mistreated by the traction company from the time the first shovelful

A crowded car in Barre heading to a baseball game near Dewey Park. *VHS.*

of dirt was overturned. The traction company, they charged, had not consulted them regarding the placement of the tracks, and in October 1897, they directed the streetcar line "to remove their trucks, poles, and other property from the streets." The dispute had to do with who was to pay for the widening of the streets where the tracks obstructed traffic. A similar issue in Montpelier delayed construction of the line there, and both matters had to be settled in court. Delays and additional expense disheartened the traction company, but Murch was able to placate town officials and resume work on the line in March 1898.

But in April, another transgression was discovered. Although their franchise prohibited the traction company from purchasing power from Jesse Viles's Middlesex hydroelectric plant, that is precisely what they intended to do. Viles's Winooski River plant was one of the largest in Vermont, and the owners of the trolley line felt that its supply of power was more reliable. Within a few years' time, their assessment would be proven incorrect. Nevertheless, later that month, workmen began stringing overhead wires to provide Viles's power to the trolley, and the laying of track in Montpelier neared completion.

By June, reported the *Argus*, an injunction to prevent the traction company from buying power from Viles's Middlesex plant was served, prompting J.J.

Flynn to comment that never had an enterprise he was involved in "been jumped on so all around unmercifully as they had in this." The Caledonia County Court in St. Johnsbury decided against the traction company and ordered the streetcar line to provide a $10,000 bond to the power company to offset any losses in its revenue. J.J. Flynn and his cohorts reluctantly complied with the directive, and the trolley line made final preparations to commence public service. Track had to be cleared of accumulated mud in Barre, and the rolling stock of six open cars, five closed cars (for winter) and a sweeper to clean snow from the tracks was made ready in the car barn.

The first commercial runs on the line commenced on June 29 in the afternoon. The newspaper reported, "The first electric car to reach this city on which fare was collected arrived at 2:15. The next car from Barre reached here at 3." The traction company planned to run cars during the afternoon and evening on that first day with forty-five minutes allowed for a one-way trip. At each end of the line, the seats on the cars were reversed for the return trip.

Within a month, additional cars were sent up Sabin Street in Montpelier to Montpelier Seminary (now Vermont College) and Washington Street in Barre. Both lines traversed severe grades. A favorite Halloween prank among boys in Montpelier was to grease the tracks with lard where they climbed Sibley Avenue and watch in glee as the car wheels spun noisily on the slippery tracks while the streetcar failed to be propelled up the hill. The main line in Barre continued down South Main Street to Jockey Hollow and the Trotting Park (where Spaulding High School is today). The Granite City boys, remembered Richard Nye, lined the tracks with torpedoes on the Fourth of July and watched the explosive progress of the trolley as it noisily made its way to City Hall Park.

Pullouts at various locations along the line allowed northbound and southbound cars to pass so cars could leave both Barre and Montpelier on the half hour. Transfers allowed passengers to board cars on the spur lines to Montpelier Seminary or the Trotting Park.

Ridership increased when the traction company added additional cars to serve special events on the route. A Montpelier band concert in July, for example, brought a great audience from Barre: "It appeared as if five sixths of the population was out, and car after car on the trolley line arrived during the evening from Barre and each was crowded to about its capacity. This increased the crowd perceptively."

As the first summer waxed full, the line appeared to prosper. In its first four weeks, the traction company had carried about sixty thousand

Washington Street in Barre. *VHS.*

passengers employing eight of its eleven cars during the day and three at night. The first car left Barre at 5:30 a.m. and arrived in Montpelier at 6:00 a.m. The last car left Barre at 10:00 p.m. and returned to the car barn after its last stop. In the first weeks of operation, the railway made improvements to its infrastructure, including erecting an office building near the car barn. Years later, this structure floated free of its foundation during the flood of 1927. Found tipped on its side, it was rescued and moved to Montpelier, where it served for decades as a dwelling at 52 Barre Street.

Eventually, Dewey Park opened on about fifteen acres two hundred yards south of the junction of Routes 2 and 302. The dance hall and picnic facilities were soon the site for family gatherings, service club picnics and beer parties attended by the granite workers from Barre and Montpelier. The park, according to Tom Borrup, was "heavily promoted and patronized during its heyday." In additional to a pavilion for dancing, a restaurant and amphitheater were constructed. A billboard promoting the park had, on its reverse, reported the *Argus*, a painting of "a trolley car at full speed with an accommodating conductor clinging to a feminine passenger with a child in her arms. Passengers are in the car windows intently watching the heroic efforts of the conductor to save her from losing the car, while the motorman is taking things easy by himself on front. The background represents three houses whose appearance is very much like those near the car barn in Berlin."

On August 3, the Ethan Allen Court of the American Order of Foresters, a fraternal society, was given the distinction of officially opening Dewey Park. Scheduled events included music by the Montpelier Orchestra (members of which were carried to the venue in a special car, playing while in transit) and a full slate of athletic contests. Extra cars were added to the trolley line at 1:00 p.m., and by 3:00 p.m., over 1,000 were in attendance. By the end of the evening, the trolley company had collected 7,000 fares, and total attendance was estimated at 3,500. The next day, the *Argus* tendered its approval: "If last night's attendance is a forerunning of what is to come, the future of the park is indeed bright. The conductors and motormen earned their pay yesterday. It was impossible for the cars to run a schedule time or to take on one trip all that wished to go, but they did their best and, to say the least handled the crowd in good shape."

The intent of providing a wholesome attraction for families was occasionally thwarted by a "rougher element of Italians from Barre" who preferred beer parties to ice cream socials. Their evening get-togethers were usually held outside the boundaries of the facility because park rules declared, "There shall be no intoxicating liquors sold in the grounds, and no immoral or demoralizing shows, concerts or tableaux shall be allowed on park grounds." Furthermore, a policeman was hired to preserve order. Park officials declared, "We intend to make it such a place as people of this city [Montpelier], Barre and Berlin will point to with pride."

By winter, the trolley line had to grapple with a new bone of contention, the snow that had to be swept from the tracks ended up in the roadway—a problem for road crews in Barre and Montpelier, who resented the additional snow removal. The snow also presented unforeseen problems on the line that provided limited service to Montpelier Seminary. The small car assigned to climb Sabin Street was not able to "develop power great enough to run through drifts of snow an inch deep," noted the *Argus*. The winter weather also curtailed activities at Dewey Park for the season, and as a consequence, the number of fares decreased precipitously.

With less income and no decline in expenses, the streetcar line decided to double its rate to ten cents. It was immediately pointed out that such an increase within city limits violated its charter. Article 15 stipulated, "The fare for riding upon the lines of said company within the city limits shall not exceed five cents and said company shall give transfer tickets to all its own lines." To comply with Article 15, the company levied the extra nickel charge when the car entered Berlin (between Dewey Park and Barre) as well as on traffic in the other direction. City fathers in both Barre and Montpelier called for a boycott of the traction line, and passengers opted instead to pay the ten-cent fare to ride the steam railroad, leaving the trolley cars empty. Montpelier city attorney F.P. Carleton insisted that the traction company provide regularly scheduled service from 5:30 a.m. to 10:30 p.m. and maintain the line up to the seminary as planned. To protest the extra charges in Berlin, two Montpelier men vowed to stay on the car after refusing to pay the additional nickel.

> *Messrs. Shay and Harvey boarded a car in this city* [Montpelier] *at 2 o'clock, paying a five cent fare. A short distance beyond the car barn Conductor Daniel Perry asked for a second fare, which they refused to pay, demanding a transfer over the remaining portion of the line.*
>
> *The conductor was in a quandary. He took the names of Shay and Harvey, and let them ride to Barre. There were several other passengers on the car at the time, two being men who immediately began to kick because they had paid their fares. One woman refused at first to pay, also demanded a transfer, but the conductor finally talked the justice of his demands to her.*
>
> *On reaching Barre the conductor went into the office of Richard A. Hoar, Attorney for the Road, for advice. He was told to put the men off the car if they refused to pay.*
>
> *Shay and Harvey returned on the same car. They paid a five cent fare, and were not asked to pay a second time. When the barn was reached the conductor alighted and explained the situation to Superintendent Smith, who called Shay and Harvey from the car. As they stepped off he motioned the conductor to go, but the two men were not going to be left so easily. They climbed on and were pulled off by Mr. Smith. Some violent language was used for a few minutes. Superintendent Smith was evidently greatly excited. The car went on without either Shay or Harvey.*

Immediately, at the conclusion of this protest, Superintendent Smith was arrested to face charges in a civil suit. Shortly thereafter, the attorney for the traction company posted notices that passengers refusing to pay the additional fare would be "put off" the cars. He also reminded the public to expect arrests in conjunction with refusing to comply, as the conductors were imbued with the authority of "Special Police" in Barre and Montpelier.

The boycott of the trolley line devastated traction company income as empty cars plied the tracks between the cities. The *Barre Telegram* reported on February 11, "A travelling man seeing the electric cars going up Main Street remarked, 'They must be running for the amusement of the boys and the frightening of the horses, judging from the few passengers seen inside.'" To further aggravate the plight of the streetcar line, central Vermont experienced heavy snows in early 1899, and as the sweeper car cleared it off the tracks, the city street workers shoveled it back on. An angry city levied fines against the streetcar line when snowbound cars failed to meet schedules, further exacerbating the woes of the electric railway. What with the weather, boycott and fines levied by the city, times were bleak for an enterprise that had seemed poised for success only months before.

It seemed that an unending spate of lawsuits and disagreements were leveled at the traction company. The construction company, which had built the line under the direction of George Murch, was, in the spring of 1899, suing to collect money it felt was owed from the original contract. One month later, John A. Roebling, the engineer who built the Brooklyn Bridge, put a lien on the traction company's real estate in an effort to collect $3,500 owed him for cable he had provided for the overhead trolley lines.

The traction company responded to its myriad troubles by replacing the superintendent of the line with Fred Andrus, brother-in-law of J.J. Flynn. Andrus hoped to placate the hostile citizenry with charm and renewed commitment to free entertainment at Dewey Park. He also installed fenders on the streetcars, which were intended to protect pedestrians from injury in the event of a collision.

The dispute over the fare increase was settled in early July with the traction company agreeing to a ten-cent fare for the months of December, January, February and March. It would be reduced to a nickel for the remaining eight months of the year. The boycott was rescinded, and the Montpelier City Council granted licenses to operate the Dewey Park dance hall and restaurant. Traffic on the streetcars resumed to pre-boycott levels, and an extra policeman was added to patrol Dewey Park. The *Argus* cited "Barre Italians" as the main reason for increasing the police presence.

While the streetcar line appeared to have resolved the problems stemming from the fare increase, a predicament beyond its control posed yet another serious dilemma. The summer of 1899 was unusually dry, and by August, there was not enough water flowing in the Winooski River to turn the turbines in Jesse Viles's hydroelectric plant. On August 20, the *Argus* wrote that the previous Sunday "was one of the most promising days the road has had this summer and it lost a great many hundred dollars in consequence of not being able to run its cars." On August 25, however, there was enough power to run two special cars to Barre to inaugurate the opening of the new Barre Opera House. The traction company decided that Viles was in breach of his contract to supply power for the trolley line and opted instead to purchase electricity from the original power company stipulated in their charter. The newly named Consolidated Power Company had installed steam turbines earlier in the summer and was ready to fill the void.

Naturally, Jesse Viles sued the traction company, but the suit languished in court until a third party bought both utilities, rendering the damages nonexistent.

The next winter, the trolley suffered two spectacular wrecks on the line that were notable for the lack of injury or death. In January, a flange broke off a wheel near the Wells and Lamson siding in Barre, and the car pitched over a fifteen-foot-high embankment. Somehow, it remained upright, and all passengers left unharmed. In February, a car on the Seminary Hill line in Montpelier encountered icy tracks on the descent to Sibley Avenue and failed to make the curve, dropping thirty feet into a snowbank, which cushioned its fall. In a "worst-case scenario," the car could have continued

A car derailed on the way to Barre near the intersection of Routes 2 and 302. *VHS.*

down the precipitous slope to Barre Street and caused serious injury. "A great many people visited the place of the accident," reported the *Argus*, "and have marveled at the narrow escape of the passengers."

As the summer season of 1900 unfolded, there was a renewed commitment to Dewey Park. The shows were free to passengers on the trolley line who had purchased a "combination ticket." The events at the park were so popular that, at times, audiences spilled out of the amphitheater onto the hillside above the wooden seats. Following is a sample review of an evening's entertainment from the *Argus*:

> *The audience was generous in its applause. First came Morrison and Berwick, a comedy sketch team, whose songs and dances met with approval. William DeLisle, boy juggler, won friends by his clever work, some of his tricks being very difficult. The Howards gave interesting dances and cake walk figures. Harry Brown, negro comedian and banjo artist caused a great deal of laughter by his jokes, some of which were given a local turn. The evening's entertainment was brought to a successful end by Minnie Shurts and Thomas Devine in Irish sketches and funny acrobatic feats.*

The offerings at the Dewey Park Amphitheater appeared to be an extension of the vaudeville stage circuit to rural Vermont, and it is not surprising that their schedule of acts was so popular. By 1901, a reliable source of electricity, seasonal fares and the popularity of entertainments at Dewey Park and the ball field down the road suggested a rosy future for the traction company, and plans were formulated for extending the lines in Montpelier. The track that climbed Sabin Street, it was reasoned, could be extended on College Street to East State Street, where it could meet the line on Main Street. While there was enthusiasm for the proposed improvements to the electric railway, nothing was done during 1901.

As the winter turned to spring in 1902, the uptick in business on the line was marred by two fatal accidents that happened in collisions with streetcars. A Mrs. Martin was thrown from her sleigh in January when her horse backed into the path of the trolley. The motorman had reacted appropriately, braking the car and lowering the fender, so no charges of negligence were proffered against him. In May, a young man from Barre, Ameila Suria, jumped from a moving car in a futile effort to retrieve his hat, which had blown away in the open vehicle. When his head hit the pavement, he suffered a fractured skull and was pronounced dead at the Barre Hospital. Despite the tragedies, the year was the most lucrative for the traction company.

The following year, 1903, dawned with labor strife. "Strike on Electric Road—When Demand for Increased Wages Was Refused Men Went Out," the headline in the *Argus* proclaimed on January 5. Workers for the traction company declared that they were unable to support their families on the small hourly salary they received. Two employees were fired when, on behalf of the hourly staff, they presented their demands to management. Soon thereafter, Mr. F.E. Weed, a representative of the Street Railway Employees of America, arrived in central Vermont, and the employees of the traction company voted for a general strike. From the beginning of operations in 1898, the conductors and motormen were paid fifteen cents an hour, but when fares declined in the winter of the first year, they accepted a temporary decrease to fourteen and three-fourths cents. As further reductions were implemented and no restoration to the fifteen-cent rate was scheduled, the men began to protest. Their demand was twenty cents an hour and a ten-hour day.

When the men voted to endorse the strike, they were promised the support of other labor unions in Barre and Montpelier, at that time a considerable portion of the labor force. The traction company was able to bring in workers from the Burlington line to keep the cars running. At a meeting of all union men in Montpelier, former mayor Sentor spoke on behalf of the striking workers, saying, "If the traction company could not afford to pay decent wages, it should be turned over to someone who could." His declaration was met with loud cheers. The public was reluctant to cross the picket lines and, once again, boycotted the electric cars. The combined support of the employees of the line, the unions in Barre and Montpelier and the public helped to find a quick resolution to the strike. By January 9, the workers accepted an hourly wage of eighteen cents for a ten-hour day, seven days a week. Additionally, the union was recognized as a bargaining unit by the company. The result was seen as a victory for the conductors and motormen, and morale among the employees was strengthened.

With the strike settled, the *Argus* made note of the workers' attitude: "They appeared as happy as a small boy with a new toy and the travelling public appeared just as well satisfied to see them out again. Several of the conductors hummed 'In the Good Old Summertime,' although the thermometer was down around zero. They were kept busy all day waving their hands at friends and sympathizers. The electric road boys had many friends."

Seemingly beset by opposition at every turn, the trolley line never achieved the commercial viability envisioned by its investors when it received its charter in 1897. Its attempts to raise fares were met with protests and

A Bailey Avenue car in Montpelier. *VHS.*

On lower State Street in Montpelier. *VHS.*

boycott. Its efforts to curtail the less profitable routes on its lines resulted in fines from the cities with which it had entered agreements and, finally, it now had to bargain with a union—a union that seemed to have the sympathies of its patrons.

Eventually, there were new competitors. A jitney, or bus service, was introduced that could compete for passengers without having to maintain tracks or pay a conductor. F.A. Jewett's Yellow Bus Line could easily traverse routes unavailable to the trolley cars. The appearance of automobiles also reduced the number of riders on the lines, and by 1925, the Barre and Montpelier Traction Company was in receivership with an auction scheduled to settle its debts. The sale placed the line in the hands of Jewett, who planned to scrap the enterprise and, thus, eliminate competition for his busses.

Shareholders intervened, however, and the trolley was able to continue to operate, but at the same time, the Vermont Public Service Board gave the Yellow Bus Line permission to compete directly with the streetcars. It is probable that this would have sounded the death knell for the traction company had not the flood of 1927 decimated the tracks and sealed its doom.

Montpelier's Dorman Kent, ever the master of understatement, put it this way: "The Jewett Bus commenced operations between here and Barre and within a week the poor old trolley line which had been gasping its last gasps for a long time was put out of business forever by extreme moisture."

Emma Goldman and Montpelier's Socialist Hall

Anarchists in the Capital City, circa 1905

It was as unlikely a parade as ever marched down Montpelier's Main Street. Emma Goldman and her partner, Dr. Ben Reitman, had arrived at the Eagles Hall at 26 State Street, and although they had a contract to rent the facility for September 5, 1909, the fraternal order had, at the last moment, refused to allow them its use. The assembled throng, numbering well over one hundred, proceeded down the main thoroughfare of the capital city to Montpelier's Socialist Hall at the corner of Barre and Granite Streets.

The Socialist Hall in Barre (today, affectionately called the Old Labor Hall) is very well known to residents of central Vermont. But few recall that Montpelier's immigrant community had similar political leanings, espoused socialist and anarchist views and even had their own Socialist Hall.

Refused use of the Eagles Hall, Emma returned to her room at the Montpelier House (100 State Street) while her manager, Reitman, according to the *Vermont Watchman*,

> *started to find another hall, but everyone whom he approached on the subject refused point blank to aid him. Finally he called at the police station and applied for a license so that Miss Goldman could speak on the street. Mayor Dawley was sent for as was Grand Juror Burton Bailey and a consultation was held in Chief J.S. Durkee's office the result of which was a hall on Barre Street was procured and another trip was made to the hotel for Miss Goldman whither she had gone.*

Emma Goldman returned to the Montpelier House Hotel. *PH.*

> *A crowding, laughing boisterous mob followed her through the streets until finally, all that could climbed aboard a street car, while the rest followed on foot.*

Montpelier's Socialist Hall was, at best, a makeshift affair at one end of Giulio Bianchi's stone shed that, according to the *Watchman*, contained a poolroom and some rough benches. The first arrivals exited the trolley car and "made themselves comfortable while waiting for the rest of the crowd and to allow the doctor [Reitman] to distribute his literature."

Giulio Bianchi built his granite shed after a fire in 1899 destroyed the previous structure. The new shed measured 265 feet by 75 feet with the long side parallel to Barre Street. Bianchi, born in Milan, Italy, in 1866, had immigrated to America after serving a ten-year apprenticeship as a sculptor in Italy. He worked in various granite towns in America, finally ending up in Barre at Jones Brothers. After two years there, he joined forces with Mr. Salvetti, and together they bought the business on Granite Street, specializing in statuary and carved monumental work. He soon bought out his partner, and in addition to employing sixty men, he was a committed Socialist. When Bianchi's industrial building was not in the service of cutting, carving and polishing granite, it was used as an assembly hall for the predominantly immigrant population of granite workers.

Reitman strode to the front of the meeting room and said:

> *We are sorry to disappoint you tonight by making you come so far to hear our beloved Emma Goldman, but it is always the case that the foreigners are always the first to aid our cause, the cause of justice, the cause of right and the cause that is to be a reality as it is now a dream. In Malden, Mass. some silly people who neither understood nor cared to understand us refused us their hall; the result was as here, for friends, Italian friends procured a place for Miss Goldman to give her message. As for the Eagles, if any of them tell you that I hired their hall through misrepresentation, you tell them it is a lie, and that they knew right along through nearly a week of advertising that Emma Goldman was to speak in their hall. Oh how stupid of them to think that we meant harm! Their reason for refusing it is that tenants who sublet the hall objected to it being used.*
>
> *You would suppose that the Eagles, who believe in fraternity would try to help mankind by hearing the plan of emancipation, the beautiful ideal for the brotherhood of man. Do you suppose that these Eagles knew anything about Emma Goldman or what she stands for? No. They were simply cowardly. Afraid of public opinion, afraid that people might think they favored anarchism. Friends, if you love fair play, order squareness. You cannot but denounce the attitude and action which the Eagles have taken this night.*

With that, he turned the speaker's table over to Miss Goldman. The *Watchman* reporter was spellbound by her oratory. "Comrades," she began. "The disagreeable affair which culminates in coming to this building to hear of the word which I have to bring to you of the emancipation of humanity from the bonds which now bind it and of the great land of peace and quiet that will come with Anarchism, is in contrast to the actions of the Eagles of this city, who while screaming for law are the first to break it." It is likely that she was surprised at the hostile reaction of the Eagles, for just three years before, she had mounted the stage at the nearby Barre Opera House with the notorious anarchist Luigi Galleani and held an enthusiastic audience spellbound for hours with her rhetoric. More recently, on the previous evening, Goldman and Galleani again spoke in Barre at a small hall in the Miles building.

Emma Goldman was the premier spokesperson for anarchism in America and, in Montpelier that evening, discarded her prepared speech. Instead, she seized the opportunity to delineate the essentials of her philosophy:

Emma Goldman. *Library of Congress.*

It is a beautiful dream, a dream fit only for the highest intellect and mind. Anarchism does not mean death nor bloodshed to humanity, but it does mean death and it does mean blood for the institutions of today…If you want to know what anarchism really is you must study modern science to which the subject is closely related, the theory of social development from the individual unit and then upward…Social beings are never at war in the individual state, and it is only collectively and by unnatural means that this blood of the brother is shed. Anarchism means freedom—absolute,

> *unconditional freedom. That is anarchy. It means that there shall be no constraint of law upon the soul or body of the man and no duty except the duty to one's self.*
>
> *The greatest hindrance to anarchy is property. This is an institution which benefits only those who are so fortunate as have grasped it from their fellow man, while he, the loser, starves, with a brother in plenty, lounging in lassitude by his side, sees nothing. The criminal code is also decidedly wrong, for in the eyes of the law, only the man proved guilty is a criminal. If you are not caught you are an honest citizen. I sneer at such a system with its illogical sequences that will allow a man to steal a railroad and be elected to high office while the petty thief is imprisoned.*

There are no further reports of Emma Goldman or Ben Reitman visiting Montpelier or, for that matter, Barre. The following evening, she attempted to continue her lecture tour in Burlington but was turned away when two policemen barred the entrance to the hall. Ben Reitman had originally rented city hall for Miss Goldman's presentation, but when they arrived in Burlington, they learned that Mayor James Burke had summarily rescinded the contract. Reitman immediately secured the use of Perleman's Hall at the corner of Cedar and Lafountain Streets and hastily prepared placards announcing the change in venue. Across the top was emblazoned the question, "Is there really free speech and fair play in Burlington?" When Goldman and Reitman arrived at the hall at 7:00 p.m., they were greeted by Mayor Burke and two policemen who barred their way. Instead, Burlington mayor Burke took the stage and, "in the name of the city of Burlington, law and society, refused permission for the anarchist to speak." Disappointed, Goldman and Reitman returned to the Van Ness House, where they were staying.

Goldman continued to proselytize for her causes: anarchism, feminism and pacifism. In 1917, she was arrested for urging young men not to register for the draft for World War I and sentenced to two years in prison. Upon her release in 1919, she was deported.

The Bianchi stone shed stood on the same lot along Barre Street for many years, bearing mute testimony to the radical political discourse in Montpelier in the first years of the twentieth century. It was last owned by the Desilets Granite Company and was razed in 2004 to make room for condominiums.

Dorman B.E. Kent

Montpelier Historian and Humorist

On the road from Kent's Corner to Maple Corner in the town of Calais, a towering pine tree looms into view. It was planted in front of the family home of Dorman Bridgeton Eaton Kent to mark the day of his birth—November 1, 1875. It still soars overhead and measures the legacy of one of Montpelier's more memorable characters: a consummate raconteur and chronicler of local history, as well as a mordant wit.

Dorman was the great-grandson of Remember Kent, an early pioneer and founder of a great Vermont family. Remember Kent brought his family to Calais in 1798 to join the first settlers in building a new town. Erecting a log cabin at what would become known as Kent's Corner, Remember married Rachel Bliss, a local woman with whom he fathered eight children and, in addition to the arduous work of subsistence farming, served as an officer in the local militia.

His son Abdiel, Dorman's grandfather, was born in 1805 and was, at various times, a mason, a schoolteacher, a shoemaker and, perhaps most notably, an innkeeper. In 1837, he completed construction of the central Vermont landmark, the Kent Tavern, to take advantage of traffic on the new road from Montpelier to the northern border that ran directly through Kent's Corner. Some ten miles from the capital of Vermont, it was a popular place to rest tired horses and travelers. The ever-resourceful Abdiel fired bricks in his own kiln and imported granite from Barre, seventeen miles distant, for the foundation, lintels and other fittings. Lumber was procured from the nearby sawmill. The oldest operating mill in Vermont is there still.

Kent's forge provided the hardware and nails, making his hotel a model of self-sufficiency.

Abdiel did not wed until he was forty years old, marrying Fanny Curtis in 1846. His four children with Fanny included Murray, Dorman's father who was born on July 15, 1847. Fanny lived just nine years after her marriage to Abdiel, passing away when Murray was eight years old. By then, there were

Murray Kent depicted in *The Auctioneer* by Thomas Waterman Wood. *Wood Art Gallery.*

many descendents of Remember Kent living in Vermont, and most, if not all, were related. In later years, many achieved positions of importance such as industrialist Atwater Kent, who was a pioneer in the early days of radio. Ira Richardson Kent achieved renown as publisher of the *Youth's Companion*, and his wife, Louise Andrews Kent, was a beloved Vermont personage, writing under the name Mrs. Appleyard. Murray's mother, Fanny, was the niece of Dorman Bridgeton Eaton, a well-known financier who later became a political operative in Washington, D.C. He was also Dorman Kent's namesake.

Murray attended school in Maple Corner and, later, Jacob Spaulding's highly regarded Barre Academy. He dabbled in business before joining his father on the farm and married Ruth Bennett of Calais. Their son, Dorman Bridgeton Eaton Kent, was born in 1875, and when Dorman was thirteen years old, Murray moved his family to Montpelier, where he built a home on Kent Street—a new neighborhood near Montpelier Seminary.

In Montpelier, Murray ran a livery stable, made harnesses and established himself as a successful auctioneer. He is portrayed in that occupation in a famous painting, *The Auctioneer*, by Montpelier artist Thomas Waterman Wood. It is notable that Wood also painted a portrait of Murray's father, Abdiel, which is in the collection of the Vermont Historical Society.

Ruth Bennett Kent's father, P.S. Bennett, achieved some immortality from the inscription on his tombstone in the East Calais cemetery. It reads, "P.S. The Old Nuisance." Dorman's old friend Harold Dwinell wrote in 1962, "The legend is that as a widower in his later years P.S. lived with a school teacher daughter. She arrived home one day to find her aged father had purchased a new high-powered rifle. Her offhand comment 'Why you old nuisance,' prompted him to reply, 'I will put those words where you can always see them.' He ordered his monument and had the inscription cut into the shaft."

Dorman's childhood in Montpelier was prosaic. Dwinell recalled,

> *He enjoyed reading and quite likely it was history he read most. If he had any favorite activity it could well have been with horses. The Kents were quite famous for owning good horses, and after moving to Montpelier, Dorman frequently drove to Kent's Corner. It is easy to believe that Dorman presented a striking appearance driving into the community sitting very straight with his derby hat and duster coat in a shiny patent leather trimmed bicycle wheeled buggy drawn by a white horse equipped with the latest trappings.*

In Montpelier, Dorman continued the education he had commenced in 1881 at a district school in Calais. Upon graduation from Union School, he attended Montpelier Seminary, completing the undergraduate degree in 1894. After further study in a business curriculum, Dorman joined his father at the livery stable on East State Street near Pitkin Court. In a year's time, at age twenty-one, he left his father's employ to join the staff of the National Life Insurance Company, the employer he would remain with for the rest of his working life. At that time, the insurance company employed thirty-eight workers and occupied the red stone building on State Street that now houses the Vermont Department of Agriculture. At almost the same time, he inherited a relatively substantial sum from his uncle Dorman Bridgeton Eaton—an amount that made marriage and a family a comfortable possibility.

Dorman found happiness in his 1904 marriage to Sarah Thompson. By 1907, he had moved Sarah and son Bennett to a home at 8 Kent Street, where their second son, Richard, was born. Dorman prospered with the success of National Life and enjoyed increasingly more responsible positions. His long tenure with the prosperous insurance company made Dorman the logical choice to compile the institutional history of the firm in celebration of its seventy-fifth anniversary in 1925.

By that time, he had joined the Vermont Historical Society and was named its librarian, serving in that capacity for almost twelve years. He also, at various times, served as secretary/treasurer, president and curator. Harold Dwinell observed:

> *Dorman was probably most widely known as a historian and he had memorized an astonishing volume of historical facts and lore, mostly about Montpelier and Washington County, but in a large degree throughout Vermont as well. The foundation and fundamental background of historical interest however, was his interest in people. Everyone whom he ever knew, it seems like, became the subject of personal research in his mind as to the person's family, what he did, when he was born, what his father did, who his mother was, etc. Fiction did not interest him. He had to know about real people.*

The late VHS director Weston Cate said of him, "Probably no member of the society ever cared more about the society than Dorman Kent. Three years after joining the society, he became librarian, a position he held for eleven years. During those years, his diary shows that his work for VHS

The Kent home on Kent Street in Montpelier. Murray Kent is pictured in a boater. *VHS.*

was central to his life, and he continued to be active in society affairs for an additional thirty-five years."

About this time, Kent became interested in genealogy and was instrumental in the decision of the Vermont Historical Society to concentrate on building a nationally recognized collection in this area. In due course, he compiled a substantial history of the Kent family. While working on his genealogy, he began collecting photographs, first of members of the Kent family, and then of anyone he knew or heard about. He bought a camera and developed an important collection of images of people in and around central Vermont. Dwinell notes:

> *He searched for pictures in attics and auctions, in antique stores, and traveled miles to find people who could identify them. His collection numbered many thousand pictures of men, women, and children who lived in Vermont and northern New Hampshire. Every picture and snapshot was identified not only with names, but also with notes about the persons or groups. The tragedy is that his collection was destroyed in the burning of the barn on Elm Street where he stored many of his goods when he gave up his home.*

Dorman Bridgeton Eaton Kent. *VHS.*

Dwinell is only partly right in lamenting the loss of Kent's acquisitions in that terrible fire. Many researchers who have used the collections at the Vermont Historical Society are indebted to Kent for the photographs that survived the conflagration—many singed, scorched or discolored by the flames. "No person ever lived," remarked Dwinell, "who knew so many people and so much about their ancestry and grandparents. Because of this he was called on to write many obituaries for the *Montpelier Argus.*"

Kent also, in the 1930s, wrote a regular column for the *Montpelier Argus*, "Events of this Day," which compiled historical facts about central Vermont in almanac form. These columns were collected and indexed in 2005 by

Montpelier native Michael Doyle. This collection is an indispensible reference for anyone interested in the history of Vermont's capital city.

It is likely that the inheritance Kent received from Dorman Bridgeton Eaton in 1900 allowed him to indulge his interests in collecting and writing about local history. Although, by current standards, $10,000 might not seem like a substantial legacy, in today's dollars it would amount to nearly $300,000—enough to buy a home and ensure a mortgage-free future. He also received eight thousand books—a number larger than the holdings of many libraries at that time.

Kent was a favorite speaker for local historical societies and clubs and often gave copies of his speeches to the Vermont Historical Society, where they are preserved to this day. He also wrote articles for the *Vermonter*, a state magazine that was published from the late nineteenth century through 1939. One example of Kent's writing style is preserved in a monologue he performed at the ceremony celebrating the seventy-fifth anniversary of the founding of National Life. The venerable insurance company had been founded in 1850 and by 1925 had grown to be a titan in the industry. One can imagine Kent assuming the guise of the Vermont rube and accentuating his Yankee twang as he read the following excerpt:

> *The railroad had just come inter Montpelier in 1850. There wan't no electric lights, gas lights, rolled stockins, jazz tunes, telephones, automobiles, cigarettes, phonographs, movies, painted women, republican party, mail deliveries, pettin' parties, water system, 18th amendment, cement walks, women's rights, bobbed hair, paved streets, daily papers, coal fires or $300 coon skin coats ter sell ter $20 a week stenographers, and everybody was happy and contented.*
>
> *In 1850 my grandfather changed his shirt about every Sunday morning—if he happened ter think of it and two shirts a year wuz more than my grandfather actually needed. In them simple but good times he wore calf skin boots at a dollar and a half a pair, which he greased up when he went ter the village, ter church, or ter a funeral.*
>
> *The rest of the time them boots wuz plastered with cow's milk—and other products of the cow, and he wuz happy. He wore his hair long and my grandmother made him one suit of clothes a year and she loved him. The cloth in one of his suits set him back about six dollars. When he tuk cold he swallered a rip roarin' snorter of rum, my grandmother rubbed his neck with goose oil and bear's grease, and he went ter bed and fergot all about it.*

In 1925 I change my shirt every other day and I ain't no dude by a damned sight. My shoes cost $7.00 a pair. I have to get my hair cut every two weeks ter keep up with the women.

When I ketch cold I don't lift in no rum, mainly because I can't afford it, but I go to a doctor who looks wise, runs a glass tube down my neck, counts my pulse, asks me what in Hell I've been up to now, *gives me 15 pills that cost him half a cent a piece and raise Sam Hill with my insides, charges me $1.50 and I go ter bed and* try *to fergit it. Where is the improvement there?*

Dorman Kent in later years. *VHS.*

It is good to remember that Dorman Kent was no stranger to big-city sophistication. He often visited relatives in Boston, New York and Washington. But he also knew that playing the part of the wise fool—in the tradition of Mark Twain and Bret Harte—was an effective way to make a point.

By 1934, Dorman's reputation had grown to the point where he was asked to record a series of broadcasts for WDEV that were sponsored by National Life. Over 1,600 fifteen-minute vignettes were produced dealing with local history and reminiscences. Sadly, none have survived.

His good friend Harold Dwinell recalled Dorman's last years:

> *Better than 6 feet tall, unusually erect, wearing a derby hat, Dorman was a familiar and easily recognizable figure on the streets of Montpelier. Everyone knew him and greeted him. Even after his stride shortened to the length of his foot there was no stoop in his posture; he held his head high. Determined, and with a sort of devil-may-care aggressiveness, he met the opposition. If the sidewalk had not been plowed out he would take to the middle of the street as if it were made for pedestrians. During his later years his health gradually failed. At least twice he fell, requiring hospitalization. For several years he was cared for at the Capital Nursing Home on Barre Street.*

As Dorman became less independent, he gave up his home on Kent Street, storing his valuable collections of Montpelier and Vermont History in a barn on Elm Street. While he was in the nursing home, a disastrous fire destroyed the barn and most of its contents.

He entered the hospital for a cataract operation in July 1951. He did not survive the operation. At the time of his death, he was still on the payroll of National Life as a consultant. He had been employed there for fifty-five years.

Thankfully, the pine tree in Kent's Corner still stands—a reminder of the devoted resident of Montpelier who took pains to record everything he could about the town he loved.

Montpelier's New Firehouse, 1924

The Consequences of a Tragic Fire

It was the worst fire in the history of Montpelier. Eleven died, and seven suffered serious injuries on the night of February 15, 1924, in the heart of the city's business district. Policemen in their offices in city hall were first to report the flames licking at the building across the alley. The fire was observed at 2:15 a.m. when visitor John Forbes, who had stopped by on his way home from work, glanced out a window and noticed flames in the Lawrence Block bursting through his own apartment. Erected in 1896, the block was situated across the alley from city hall on the lot now occupied by the Rite-Aid Pharmacy. As a police officer hurried to the alarm box at the corner of Main and Barre Streets, Forbes raced to the building next door to rescue his wife.

The Lawrence Block, built of brick, was one of the largest in Montpelier, standing four stories high. The street floor was devoted to stores, the second to offices and the third and fourth to apartments. The building was owned by the estate of Asa Blanchard, well known for the Blanchard Block, which still stands near the corner of Main and East State Streets, north of city hall.

The fire began in the offices of Peck Brothers Hardware, engendered by an overheated chimney, and rapidly spread throughout the structure. When the fire truck arrived, its ladder was insufficient to reach the top floor of the building, and deaths resulted from victims jumping from the building and missing the nets held by firemen on the ground. Some landed in the nets only to suffer severe injury when the force of their fall could not be

Lawrence Block decorated for Dewy Day, 1899. *VHS.*

countered by the men holding the nets. It was also later discovered that the door to some of the fire escapes had been locked.

Initial reports were, as is often the case, wrong. The *Boston Herald* reported that an explosion started the blaze and that "firemen sent to an old barn in which the ladder truck was stored found the machine frozen to the ground and the barn doors coated with ice, which they had to chop away before they could move the truck." While this rumor persisted in spite of accounts to the contrary, it was without foundation, according to an official report issued on February 26 by state's attorney Charles Adams and fire marshal A.G. Preble. The initial report that an explosion started the conflagration was also discredited by investigators. The explosion noticed by witnesses was due to an infusion of oxygen into the already burning structure.

Police officer Edgar Sloan tendered the first alarm by telephone but also ran to the street to send an alarm from a street box. "The fire whistle shrieked a single round and then went silent, though the bells continued to ring."

Fire chief Vaney Persons, accompanied by five firemen, was upon the scene at once with a small truck and hose wagon from the small station around the corner on East State Street. The firemen soon realized that the shrieking forms that appeared in the windows were residents of the building. They also realized that the ladders on their pumper were too short to reach the top two stories of the Lawrence Block.

"Call firemen responded to the alarm and manned life nets into which men and women jumped, but they could not hold the nets off the ground. Other firemen were sent running to the old city barn a quarter of a mile away to drag back the old ladder truck, but they had lost many minutes and, in that time, lives had been lost," reported the *Argus*.

The "Call Firemen" were part-time employees of the fire department who were summoned when needed and paid for the hours they spent on the job. Bob Snetzinger, retired Montpelier fireman and unofficial historian of the MFD, recalled that the department had only had paid staff since 1911. The old ladder truck was a horse-drawn vehicle kept with the horses at the City Barn on Prospect Street across the Winooski River. Snetzinger pointed out that the men sent for this vehicle first had to harness the horses, then attach them to the truck and then drive the horses to the fire. It was a time-consuming procedure. Within three weeks after the fire, a Ford tractor was purchased to replace the horses. It could "climb the steepest hills of the city and reach speeds of 18 miles per hour," reported the *Argus*.

> *Walter C. Washburn, leading Mason and prominent in the insurance business, leaped from an upper story toward an outstretched life net, but he miscalculated and jumped wide. He was dashed to death on the ice-covered sidewalk.*
>
> *Mr. Washburn's entire life was spent in this city. He was educated in the schools here and went into the insurance business with his father several years ago. Mr. Washburn was the general distributor of Fleishman's Yeast here and in Barre. He was also Past Potentate of Mount Sinai Temple*

in this city. Mrs. Washburn and their ten-months-old daughter Jean, are counted among the missing. They were later recovered and the entire family received funeral rites at the same time. Mrs. Washburn and her infant daughter occupied the same casket.

Mrs. Emma Waterman jumped into space and struck the sidewalk, her fall partially broken by the net.

Firemen picked her up and carried her into city hall, which had been transformed into a makeshift emergency room. She died a few minutes later. As the injured were recovered from the building, they were transported to Heaton Hospital as fast as the ambulance could make the trip.

As word of the fire made its way around the city, a large crowd gathered at the scene of the conflagration in the dark hours before daybreak. Many volunteered to work alongside police and fireman to search for bodies through the charred detritus. The *Argus* reported that "the men searching the ruins found many items of value such as rings, watches, silverware and jewelry." Under the debris of Peck Brothers Hardware store, knives, revolvers and guns recovered from the ashes were taken charge of by police. The newspaper also reported that the Grand Union Tea Company was planning to reopen as soon as a suitable space could be secured.

John Forbes, who first discovered the blaze and rushed to rescue his wife, also carried his father-in-law, William Harvey, to safety. Another hero was resident William Grisborn, who returned to the smoke-filled hall to rescue others but finally was overcome with the lack of oxygen and died beside his wife. Dorman Kent, avid chronicler of Montpelier's past remarked:

Will Grisborn, who occupied an apartment in that block was one of the first to awake. The apartments were filled with black smoke but he and his wife might have escaped as did a few who were first awakened but Will saw his chance and he took it. Instead of leaving the burning building, which he could have easily done, he rushed from apartment to apartment calling people up and more than one person owed his or her life to the efforts of Will Grisborne. He did not get out and certainly he gave up his life for others.

His remains were positively identified by his watch. The body found near his was assumed to be that of his wife.

The *Argus* noted that a "factor that played against the fate of those trapped was the small number of available men to man the life net." It was necessary to jump before a sufficiently large force of call firemen could assemble to properly handle the net. "The result is when the jumpers struck the net the men handling it were unable to bounce them up in the air before they struck the ground." Bob Snetzinger had trained with the life nets as a young fireman in Montpelier. He has an appreciation for what it takes to safely break the fall of a victim leaping from a burning building. "The nets are about twelve feet in diameter, and a force of twelve men are needed to keep the net from crashing to the ground," he recalled.

As residents of the Lawrence Block felt the flames at their backs, they felt the necessity to jump before a full component of firemen were assembled to handle the net. The reports indicate that while some who jumped into nets were able to save their lives, they suffered serious injuries. Claude Martin, a station agent for the Wells River Railroad, received a fractured pelvis and a broken arm. The *Argus* pessimistically predicted, "He will probably die of his injuries." Aimie Menard received a broken back from his fall to the net, and Eda Clough broke her shoulder. Inez Dingwall made it safely out of the burning building only to slip and fall on the ice, breaking her hip.

The firemen were able to contain the blaze despite fears that it might spread to nearby city hall. One innovation was reported in the firefighting effort. Bright searchlights were installed by the Montpelier and Barre Electric Light and Power Company to assist the search for bodies during the long winter night. "Tonight their glare illuminates the whole scene of horror," reported the *Montpelier Argus*. The description continued:

> *Those present will never forget the exciting and maddening screams in the first few minutes following the alarm. The occupants of the building, with the exception of those able to make their way to fire escapes, opened their windows and screamed loudly and frantically for help, imploring that ladders be laid up to them. Seeing that the ladders were not forthcoming they had to venture the long jump to the life nets. Hesitating before taking the frightful plunge, they would hold back and lie on the window sills contemplating the dizzy depths into which they must leap and the possibility of a slight miscalculation that would smash them to pieces on the ground; then in desperation they would let go and jump into the net. Others who had decided to jump grew more and more frantic at the delays while others were jumping and would cry piteously for aid. It was one of the most heartbreaking scenes in the history of the city.*

The fire burned for almost two hours until nothing remained but the brick walls and an "immense mass of blackened, smoking timbers and steel beams

Lawrence Block fire, 1924. *VHS.*

glowed red hot." As soon as it was practical, a search party composed of employees of the telephone and electric companies, the city and the fire department entered the ruins shortly after noon on the next day. The brick walls of the Lawrence Block had that morning been reduced to a single story to minimize the danger of collapse. A cable had been attached to the front wall and hooked to the undercarriage of an automobile, and the upper stories collapsed into Main Street, which had been closed by the police.

Almost immediately after the fire was contained, an investigation was ordered by state's attorney Adams and fire marshal Preble. They set up temporary offices at nearby city hall and began questioning firemen who were first at the scene. Owners and proprietors of stores in the Lawrence Block were also called in for questioning, as were surviving residents.

Despite initial criticisms leveled at the fire department, its efforts were praised in the aftermath of the tragedy. "All those who would criticize and start and spread rumors of inadequacy and negligence are unthinking and unkind," stated J.P. Gallaher of the local Red Cross chapter, who had nothing but admiration for the stalwarts who braved subfreezing temperatures in attempts to rescue the victims. "The work they were suddenly called upon to do in the middle of the night was so far beyond their experience and beyond their strength that we feel no department could have done more."

Montpelier's annual Winter Carnival scheduled for the following week was canceled, and the Montpelier Ski Club asked that all merchants displaying posters promoting the event remove them. "The fire is the worst in Montpelier's history and has cast gloom over the entire city," lamented the newspaper.

Fire chief Persons had repeatedly warned of the consequences of not having a centralized department in Montpelier, but his pleas had fallen on deaf ears until the tragedy of the Lawrence Block fire. Firefighting equipment had been distributed to various locations around the city leading to delays as remote pumpers were dispatched to the scene of a fire. Not surprisingly, the voters approved a new central fire station at the city's annual meeting held just a few weeks after the fire. Bonds worth $100,000 were sold to finance a modern fire department.

By February 4, 1925, a new firehouse would occupy the Main Street location now so familiar to the residents of the capital city. A dispute over the locations beside and behind city hall ended in favor of the site that was already owned by the city.

An official grand opening, some months after the building had been in use, was celebrated on April 29, 1925. The high school orchestra provided music, and boys from Main Street School ushered guests and served punch and cookies while residents were welcomed to their new firehouse. The *St. Albans Messenger* reported:

> *On the ground floor they were permitted to examine the apparatus which included the large hook and ladder truck* [a new motorized vehicle], *the triple combination, the combination, and the Ford truck.*

The new firehouse on Main Street, 1925. *PH.*

> *A very interesting feature was the old hand pump that was on display. This horse-drawn pump, in use scores of years ago, presented a telling contrast to the more modern motor driven machines.*

A decade after the horrible fire, Dorman Kent wrote of it in his almanac-like column in the *Montpelier Argus*, "Events of This Day":

> *Ten years ago today a fire occurred in this city and eleven lives were lost. I was in New York City at the time and I am thankful I did not see it. My wife told me that after she heard the fire alarm ring she looked out the window and flames thirty feet high could be seen coming out of the roof of the block. My son, Richard, who will get up about half an hour after we call him in the morning, is always on hand at night when the fire alarm rings. He can get up, get dressed and get out of the house quicker that I can count the last stroke of the fire alarm and, of course, he went to that fire. He did not stay long and his mother told me he said: "Ma, I couldn't stay any longer. People are jumping from that block and a lot of them have lost their lives."*

For a city that had known such a horrific tragedy less than a year earlier, the presence of the new station offered reassurance and, perhaps, atonement.

Mari Tomasi

The Montpelier Novelist Who Told Vermont's "Italian Story"

When Mari Tomasi died of cancer in 1965, she still resided in the house where she was born at 63 Barre Street in Montpelier. The address is significant for a couple reasons. First, it is named for the town she immortalized in much of her written work, and second, Montpelier's other great novelist, D.P. Thompson, in the nineteenth century also made his home on Barre Street, a few hundred yards from the Tomasi house. Mari is primarily known today for her second novel, *Like Lesser Gods*, as well as the compendium of oral history interviews collected for the Writers Project of the Works Progress Administration from 1938 to 1940. The Writers Project used tax dollars to employ journalists and fiction writers during the difficult years of the Depression. This important collection was published as *Men Against Granite* in 2004, a title that editor and University of Vermont (UVM) professor Alfred Rosa borrowed from Tomasi's novel *Like Lesser Gods*. These important transcriptions continue to compose an essential primary source for the history of Barre. A resurgence of interest in "immigrant literature" led to the publication of *Men Against Granite*, as well as the republication of *Like Lesser Gods*.

Despite the increased interest in her work over the past several years, Tomasi's personal life remains, to a great degree, a mystery. Her nieces, Linda and Barbara, remember a stylish woman who was so appealing that people were drawn to her. Embracing her Italian heritage, she cooked in the Piedmont tradition, and polenta was a staple on the Tomasi table. In season, she gathered wild mushrooms in the forests around Berlin Pond, and every

Mari Tomasi's backyard office. *Tomasi Family.*

fall, she harvested chestnuts from trees along the Three Mile Bridge Road. Like many in town, she picked dandelions for wine and served the greens in salads. A doting aunt, she had pet names for her nephews and nieces selected from classical mythology, remembered all their birthdays and encouraged them to speak Italian. Despite her vivacious nature, she was a devout Catholic, and religious icons and symbols were rife in the Barre Street home she shared with her family. Priests from the church down the street often came to their home to celebrate the Mass for Mari's infirm mother, and a font of holy water near their front door was refreshed weekly. Once, she even paid niece Barbara a dollar to learn the Hail Mary in Latin. She was very active in the Poetry Society of Vermont, and Berlin poet Arthur Hewitt was a great friend, kindred spirit and enthusiastic supporter of her verse.

Linda and Barbara remember family outings on Sunday afternoons in Mari's gold Studebaker and Aunt Mari working in her beautifully maintained perennial garden, where a typewriter mounted atop a stump served as her makeshift study in fair weather.

Mari's parents emigrated from Turin, Italy, to Montpelier in the early twentieth century, and she was born (as Marie) in the capital city on

Mari Tomasi. *Aldrich Public Library.*

January 30, 1907. At birth, she had a walking disability, and Mari's gait was marked by a distinctive limp. She was taken to Burlington for corrective surgery, which was partially successful, and later convalesced on a trip to Italy. Never marrying, she remained at her family home at 63 Barre Street until her death, pursuing a career as a writer and journalist. She never regretted her dedication to writing and her family. In 1959, she wrote of her choice of the single life:

> *For the past few years until her death, just eight weeks ago my mother was confined to her bed; my sister (who is a registered nurse) and I both had the wonderful, God-given privilege of caring for her. Perhaps with marriage I would have not had this privilege—I don't know. But I think it was one*

> *of God's own reasons for directing me to the unmarried state. During this period, major writing projects had to be abandoned, but I was Associate Editor of* Vermont Life *for two years, have continued a column in the* Troubadour, *the publication of the Poetry Society of Vermont, and have also continued with several writing and civic projects.*

Mari also found time to work as an editor for the *Montpelier Evening Argus* during the war years, as well as edit the *Vermont State Welfare Magazine*, compile three state legislative yearbooks and serve briefly as Montpelier's representative to the Vermont General Assembly.

Her parents, Bartolomeo and Margarita, chose Vermont for their home because the Green Mountains resembled the area around northern Italy's Lake Como and the countryside near Turin from whence they came. In Montpelier, they established a grocery and cigar store. Mari attended St. Michael's School on Barre Street. After graduation, it has been reported that she matriculated briefly at Wheaton College, but neither the Wheaton in Illinois nor the one in Massachusetts has a record of her attendance. It is known that she attended Trinity College in Burlington, a Catholic school. With Bartolomeo's death in 1926, she no longer had the resources to pay for tuition and left academia to test her ability as a writer for newspapers and magazines. Through the Poetry Society of Vermont she met Arthur Wallace "Pop" Peach, a professor at Norwich University, who recognized and nurtured her talent.

Mari's first book, *Deep Grow the Roots*, published in 1940, is set in Fascist Italy and brought her distinction as a new American novelist. The novel is a warning about the menace of Mussolini and his virulent fascist form of government. Very likely it was based on her visit to Italy. The novel had modest sales, but Mari's work was well received by the critics as a promising new voice in fiction, earning her recognition and a fellowship to the Bread Loaf Writers Conference at Middlebury College.

While working on her first novel, Mari was employed by the WPA for the Writers Project. She collected oral histories in Barre, and her work, aside from contributing important primary source material for the Granite City, instilled in her the knowledge and background of the granite industry (she collaborated on a thesaurus of terms used in the manufacture of monuments) that enabled her, with the support of a Bruce Fellowship, to write *Like Lesser Gods*, her enduring second novel that has been hailed as a significant work in the literature of Italian Americans.

Set in the fictional village of Granitetown, the setting is unmistakably Barre. The theme of immigrant assimilation is in stark contrast to the

Dust jacket for *Like Lesser Gods*. *PH.*

imminent tragedy of silicosis, the disease that sent legions of stonecutters to an early grave. This tragedy was compounded by the fact that the carvers held a great passion for their art and practiced their craft despite its mortal consequences. In the novel, Pietro, a carver, explains the dilemma to his friend Gino:

> *You have to cut it to know. It is hard stone. Beautiful. Lasting. Always when I carve a name on a memorial, I feel, well, important. I carve the name and I say to myself From up there in heaven, the* Dio *creates a new life; and when he sees fit to take it away, then we stonecutters on earth take up where He left off. We take up the chisel, we carve the name, we make a memory of that life. Almost, boy, it is being like-like-*
>
> *In Gino's mind tiptoed a sentence from an old mythology book: On Olympus lived the greater gods; and below, the lesser. He nodded to Pietro, understanding him, and he murmured quietly—"like lesser gods."*

Originally published in 1949, the book has seen two subsequent printings, first in 1988 and again ten years later. Despite a style that may seem dated to some, the book has been popular as a means of interpreting the Italian American immigrant experience and as an insight to the lives of Italian stonecutters in Barre. UVM English literature professor Alfred Rosa wrote an afterword to the 1988 edition that infers the sense of the novel:

> *Mari Tomasi was deeply aware of the treachery of the granite that brought Italians to Vermont. She knew the torture of the tuberculo-silicosis or "stonecutters TB," as it was called—that lay in wait behind the incredibly durable and stately granite. The more the workers dedicated themselves to the stone, the more they created their own figurative and literal tombstones. In a startling and profound way, Mari Tomasi realized that the granite workers continually celebrated and memorialized their own deaths in the stones they quarried and carved for others they would never know.*
>
> *As a symbol, the granite is even more interesting. It is not merely blasted, hoisted out of the earth, sawed, carved, polished, and shipped to far-off places. Certainly, the granite is reminiscent of the ice in Thoreau's Walden Pond, which in winter was cut from the top of the pond and sent all over the world. Like the ice, the granite celebrates a region but also, by its distribution, achieves a level of both actual and symbolic universality.*

The leading character of *Like Lesser Gods*, Pietro, also appears in Tomasi's short story "Stone," published in 1942. In this instance, the disease slowly compromises his health, and Pietro is admitted to a sanatorium that resembles the one that once cared for sufferers on Beckley Hill in Barre. There he dies the slow and inevitable death from silicosis but, nevertheless, is content in the satisfaction of his art.

The WPA interviews later published as *Men Against Granite* were collected primarily by Tomasi with assistance from Roaldus Richmond, whose work on the project was primarily administrative and who would also become a novelist in the genre of western fiction. Under the direction of folklorist Ben Botkin, they used a questionnaire to collect basic information from their sources and then conducted a free-ranging interview in which the informant became a storyteller. The expressed purpose of the project was to create a body of interviews that would extol the melting pot of America, featuring Barre's wide range of ethnic groups. Botkin intended the archive to combat the nationalistic fervor of fascism that had become popular in Italy and Germany. Sadly, the collection of interviews remained unpublished for more than sixty years. New Deal projects were often discredited in their time because of suspicions of the political agendas of many of the participants. Nevertheless, the fifty-two narratives that make up *Men Against Granite* evoke the Granite City in all its prewar glory.

At this time, while still working for the WPA, Tomasi also began the research that would become "The Italian Story in Vermont," a substantial nonfiction work that appeared in *Vermont History* in 1960.

In 1977, Mari's last remaining sibling, Marguerite Tomasi, was interviewed by scholar Helen Borolini. "I always called her Mary," said her sister, and that is how her name appeared in the decennial census from 1920 through 1940. The interview took place in the Tomasi family home on Barre Street. Marguerite indicated that the baptismal record at St. Augustine's Church lists her given name as Marie. But aside from basic family information, Borolini gained no more insight into the enigmatic author's life. "I asked questions, but Marguerite and the other family members present could not answer them; only that Mari had not discussed her writing in the family, had not kept a diary, had left no material for other novels." She had, however, crafted a collection of children's stories, enjoyed by her numerous nephews and nieces.

A family story that does survive suggests the attention Mari gave the children in her extended family. One day, her young brother Ernest Tomasi was fishing in the Winooski River behind the Tomasi home on Barre

This carved monument adorns the Tomasi family plot in Montpelier's St. Augustine Catholic Cemetery. *PH.*

Street. In the process of disengaging his hook, he tore a flap of skin loose from the flesh below the fish's jaw. Urgently pleading for help from Mari, who was sewing in the parlor, she helped him stitch sutures to reattach the skin, and Ernie happily returned the fish to the river. He later became a physician with the generous support of Mari to help pay his way through medical school.

Whether she is considered enigmatic or self-effacing, her work has seen a resurgence of interest among critics who study the literature of the immigrant experience. Her equal devotion to the ideals of her family and heritage as much as literature may account for the small body of work she produced in her short life. But in recent decades, her work has been read as much (if not more) as when she lived on Barre Street in Montpelier.

About the Author

Paul Heller grew up in Montpelier, attending Main Street and Montpelier High Schools. After a career as a librarian and innkeeper, he retired to take aimless walks and read and write local history. He is the author of *Granite City Tales*, *The Calais Calamity* and *The History of the Banjo*. His writings have been published in various newspapers and magazines. Paul Heller and Marianne Kotch live in Barre, Vermont.